S0-BZK-909

Other cookbooks by the author

BRIDE'S COOKBOOK

CAKES, COOKIES AND PASTRIES

CASSEROLE COOKBOOK

COMPLETE BOOK OF ORIENTAL COOKING

COMPLETE ROUND-THE-WORLD COOKBOOK

COMPLETE ROUND-THE-WORLD HORS D'OEUVRES BOOK

COOK AS THE ROMANS DO

COOKING FOR THE FREEZER

CREATIVE MEALS IN HALF THE TIME

DICTIONARY OF INTERNATIONAL FOOD AND COOKING TERMS

DIET DELIGHT COOKBOOK

FLAVOR OF SPAIN

HAMBURGER COOKBOOK

INTER-CONTINENTAL GOURMET COOKBOOK

INTERNATIONAL ENCYCLOPEDIA OF COOKING

MYRA WALDO'S CHINESE COOKBOOK

PLEASURES OF WINE

RECIPES FROM GREAT RESTAURANTS

SOUFFLÉ COOKBOOK

MYRA WALDO'S
DESSERT COOKBOOK

Myra Waldo's DESSERT COOKBOOK

Myra Waldo

The Macmillan Company, New York, New York
Collier-Macmillan Publishers, London

The Macmillan Company
866 Third Avenue, New York, N.Y. 10022
Collier-Macmillan Canada Ltd., Toronto, Ontario

Portions of this book appeared previously as *Cakes, Cookies and Pastries*, published in 1962 by Collier Books, New York.
Library of Congress Catalog Card Number: 72–93307
First Printing
Printed in the United States of America

Contents

Introduction

THE ABILITY to make fine cakes, cookies and pastries is the hallmark of the accomplished cook. Learning to bake is no longer surrounded by mystery, for over the years, science has analyzed the reasons for success (and failure) in baking. By following a set of rules, it is possible to have success in all cake-making endeavors. But the essential is that these rules be followed.

It is only in cake-making that the cook is strictly limited to the wording of the recipe. In preparing a meat casserole, for example, the cook is at liberty to add her own little touches, such as adding carrots even when the recipe does not call for them. If a recipe specifies beef broth and an unusually enterprising cook uses white wine instead, the result will of course be quite different, but not necessarily disastrous. In some cases, the cook may even use a different meat than the one called for in making a casserole, such as veal in place of beef. The finished dish may taste quite different from the one described in the recipe, and it may turn out to be good or not quite so good. But the finished casserole will be edible, in any event.

This is not true of cakes or pastries. Small variations in a recipe, even those that might seem only a matter of personal taste or creative expression, could easily result in a poor cake, sometimes even a downright inedible failure. It is impossible to get successful results if the recipe is merely used as a starting point or springboard for a freewheeling expression of the cook's personality, as is commonly done in making appetizers, soups, fish, meats or salads. As with all recipes, but particularly those for cakes or pastries, you should read the recipe through *first*, before you do anything. It is very disconcerting to find, in the middle of making a cake, that there is no baking powder in the kitchen, for example, and substitutions are never completely satisfactory. It is always advisable to check your ingredients before taking even the first step. Cake recipes are a matter of checks and balances, of using just the right amount of leavening in proportion to eggs and flour, of the right amount of shortening in proportion to the dry ingredients. If one of these factors were to be altered, the result would probably be disappointing.

The author receives hundreds of letters each year asking why certain cakes succeed and others fail. An analysis of the complaints in these letters suggests that in ninety per cent (or more) of the cases, the difficulty lies in either reading the recipe incorrectly or in not following the instructions carefully. In the remaining cases, the trouble arises from a variety of sources, such as improperly regulated ovens, stale ingredients, ingredients combined at the wrong temperature, egg whites beaten when ice cold, and so on. But the greatest single cause of difficulty seems to stem simply from a failure to follow the recipes closely and without variation.

A cake can only be as good as the ingredients that go into it. Needless to say, truly fresh butter will make a better cake than butter which has been in the refrigerator for weeks, gradually losing its flavor; and of course, creamery butter makes a better product than does margarine. If baking powder is called for, and you use an opened can of year-old baking powder, you can expect much of its lifting qualities to be gone. A package of flour that has been left open will absorb moisture from the air on humid days and will often make a heavy, streaky cake. It is essential that all baking ingredients, such as flour or baking powder, be stored in a tightly covered container and kept away from air.

HOW TO BECOME A GOOD BAKER

1. Read the recipe over at least twice, slowly and carefully.

2. If you have any doubts about the meaning of the terms used in the recipe, look them up in the section on definitions beginning on page 5.

3. If the recipe calls for eggs, remove them from the refrigerator at least one hour before using, so that they can come up to room temperature. If they are to be separated, separate them immediately upon taking them from the refrigerator.

4. Arrange in a convenient place *all* of the ingredients called for in the cake.

5. Make sure that the pan you intend to use is the correct size; this is quite important, for an outsized pan would result in a flat cake with a texture, appearance and taste totally different from what you anticipated. A small pan would result in an over-expanded cake, which would also be unsatisfactory. Use only shiny, unspotted pans for cakes, for they reflect heat best. Pies may be baked in glass pie plates.

6. Preheat the oven at least 20 minutes in advance, so that the oven can come up to the proper temperature. Oven temperatures must be checked carefully, for thermostats frequently go out of order. Place a small oven thermometer (they may be purchased for about $1) in the oven to check the thermostat from time to time.

7. In recipes, standardized measures are used, including teaspoons, tablespoons and cups. This does not mean that you may use any handy teaspoon, tablespoon or cup in your kitchen. One ordinary household tablespoon may hold twice as much as an-

other tablespoon; it is *absolutely essential* that the standard measuring teaspoon, tablespoon and cup be used. If not, the entire balance of ingredients will be lost, and disappointment will inevitably follow.

8. Which rack in the oven should you use? Where there are no special instructions, place the cake on a rack in the middle of the oven, centering the cake as much as possible, so that heated air can circulate evenly around the cake. Don't put anything else in the oven when making a cake, for this will interfere with proper baking. It would be poor economy to bake two large cakes at the same time, only to find that neither is properly baked. However, shallow cakes may be baked a few at a time if the recipe specifically calls for it. Assuming that the average oven has two racks, dividing the oven into three levels, you should follow these general rules:

Bottom: Never use this for baking, for the bottom of the cake would be overly browned with the top remaining partially unbaked.

Middle: This is best for almost all baking, particularly unfilled pie or pastry shells.

Top: This should be used only to brown quickly, or caramelize, the tops of cakes. Ordinarily, baking on the top rack would produce cakes which are too brown on top and unbaked on the bottom.

9. The baking time specified in each recipe can only be approximate because of the many variables (freshness of leavening, temperature variations in ovens, amount of kneading, etc.). It is quite essential that cakes be tested shortly before the end of the baking time specified. This is done best with a "cake tester" or a long toothpick or wooden match. If dough adheres to the cake tester or toothpick, the cake is not done. The tester should come out "clean," or almost dry. Another test is to press the cake gently with your finger; the cake should spring back quickly. If your finger leaves an impression on the surface, the cake is not done.

10. The recipes in this book are best suited for altitudes from sea level to 3,000 feet. If you live at a higher altitude, you will have to make a few allowances. First, because flour becomes drier and more compact at high altitudes, you should use slightly less of it than the recipe calls for. Second, you should use yeast somewhat sparingly since yeast action is stronger at high altitudes. Third, you should increase your baking temperature very slightly: for example, if the recipe calls for 350°, make it 360°. However, high-altitude baking varies somewhat from recipe to recipe, and only by experimenting will you find the correct allowances for a given cake or pastry.

11. To cool the cake, place the pan on a cake rack, so that air can circulate on all sides; if the cake is placed on a counter or other solid surface, no air can circulate under the bottom of the cake, and it will cool unevenly, with undesirable results. Unless otherwise directed, let the cake cool for about 15 minutes, then loosen the sides gently from the pan with a spatula. Then remove the cake rack from under the cake pan, and place the rack on top of the pan. Invert quickly, holding cake rack and cake pan together, remove the pan, and let the cake cool further.

DEFINITIONS OF BAKING TERMS

Bake: Cook in a heated oven.

Beat: Incorporate air into ingredients. When the ingredients are soft (like egg whites), this is best done by means of an electric mixer, a rotary beater or a wire whisk. When the ingredients are firm (like a batter), the beating is best done with an electric mixer or with a wooden spoon.

Blend: Mix together two or more ingredients until combined.

Chill: Place in a refrigerator until cold to the touch.

Cream: Soften butter (or other shortening); it may be done with a kitchen spoon or by electric mixer. Sometimes two or more ingredients are creamed together, that is, softened and mixed together at the same time.

Cut in shortening: Use two knives (or a special kitchen tool called a "pastry blender") in a crisscross fashion to cut the shortening so that it combines with the flour, in that way causing the formation of flour-covered particles of fat. Hands cannot be used because their natural body warmth would interfere with the process.

Dot: Place small bits of an ingredient (usually butter) on the surface of the cake being prepared.

Fold in: Incorporate air into a mixture while combining the ingredients. This process is extremely important, for if air is not incorporated into the mixture, the cake will not rise properly. The process: First (in the absence of other, specific instructions), put the batter in a fairly large bowl. Next, pile the beaten egg whites lightly on top of the batter. Use a wire whisk, a large spoon or a spatula, and *very gently and slowly* bring the whisk (or spoon or spatula) downward into the mixture and then upward to make a complete circular motion. As you do this, some of the batter will be lifted out onto the egg whites, and on the downward motion some of the egg whites will be mixed into the batter. Continue this until the ingredients are reasonably well mixed together. The egg whites need not be completely combined with the batter; some patches of egg whites may be visible. It is important, however, that the folding process be done slowly and gently.

Grease: Spread butter, margarine or oil on a surface, such as a cooky sheet, muffin cup, etc.

Knead: Handle dough to bring it to a desired consistency. If the dough has some firmness or consistency to begin with, it is best kneaded on a board, although any flat surface will do. Lightly sprinkle flour on the surface. Flour the hands lightly, then flatten the dough just a little and shape into a ball. (The dough will be somewhat flat on top.) Fold the dough in half, and using the heel of the hand, press down and away from you, then fold over and press down again. Each time, turn the dough to the left, so that you are always kneading a different part of the dough. Keep this up until the dough is elastic, smooth and satiny. This should take from 8 to 10 minutes. It may be necessary to use a bit more flour on the surface or on the hands when the dough becomes sticky. If the unkneaded dough is very soft or sticky, it may be advisable to knead the dough in a bowl.

Preheat: Allow the oven temperature to reach a desired degree of heat in advance; this usually requires about 20 minutes.

Roll out dough: Form and thin the dough. If the dough has been refrigerated, remove 10 minutes before using to allow it to soften a little; however, it cannot remain at room temperature much longer than 10 minutes or the dough will become soft and tacky and difficult to work with. Form the dough by hand into a rectangle or any other desired shape. Dough may be rolled on any large flat surface, although a piece of marble is probably the best. A table top or a pastry cloth may also be used, in which case a very small amount of flour should first be sprinkled on the flat surface and also on the rolling pin. (Another technique is to roll dough out between two sheets of waxed paper, in which case no flour need be used.) Roll out fairly lightly *in one direction only*—away from you. Lift up the rolling pin and roll again. After every few rolls, turn the dough a quarter turn so that the longer dimension of the rolled dough now extends from left to right. Continue rolling until the dough is the proper thinness. Use as little flour as possible, although a small additional amount may be required to keep the dough from sticking to the board or to the rolling pin. It is not necessary to press down very hard to roll dough properly unless the dough is too cold.

Scald: Heat liquids to just below the boiling point. In scalding, a typical formation of bubbles appears around the outside edges but not in the middle of the saucepan.

Stir: Mix together ingredients until well-blended, using a spoon. Do not stir too long. You should stop just as soon as the ingredients are combined.

Whip: Beat speedily, usually cream or egg whites, to add air and increase the volume of the ingredients.

BAKING INGREDIENTS

Flour: There are many different kinds of flour on the market, and this profusion might call for a degree of caution among cakemakers. Standard flour, called "all-purpose," may in general be used for any recipe in this book, unless otherwise specified. However, it does result in a somewhat more coarsely textured cake than "cake flour" would, the latter being made from a soft variety of winter wheat. The difference, though, is not particularly discernible when cakes are made with eggs; in this case, all-purpose flour is often satisfactory. Self-rising flours are those which already contain baking powder and salt; they are not generally recommended, but if you use them, omit the leavening and salt from the recipe.

Flour should be sifted before using, even though the flour is labeled "pre-sifted," because as moisture accumulates, the flour loses some of its packaged (original) qualities.

Sift all flour first, then measure.

Baking powder: All recipes in this book require the type of baking powder called "double-acting," which means that the baking powder has two rising actions. The first takes place when the powder is mixed with a liquid, causing a partial formation of gas;

the second rising occurs when the batter is heated, causing the gas to expand and resulting in a more evenly leavened product.

Shortening: Butter makes the best cakes, but margarine may be used with results that are almost as good. The hydrogenated (solid) shortenings may be used, but flavor changes may be expected, for these hydrogenated shortenings are flavorless. Salad oil may be used whenever melted shortening is called for, but the results may be somewhat different. Lard has a strong flavor, and bakers unfamiliar with its taste might do well to avoid its use in cakes. Lard can be used for pie pastry, however. All in all, there can be no doubt that butter or margarine is the best shortening for making fine cakes and pastry.

Eggs: There is little or no difference between brown and white eggs. If the recipe calls for eggs, see that they are fresh; stale eggs tend to deteriorate, causing a lessening of flavor and therefore a poorer taste in the finished cake. Refrigerate eggs until you are ready to use them; if the recipe calls for separated eggs, separate them immediately upon removal from the refrigerator. Then allow them to stand at room temperature for 1 hour before using. Egg whites will beat up properly only at room temperature, but eggs separate best when cold. When whole eggs are added to a recipe, add them one at a time, unless instructions call for prebeating.

What size egg should you use in a recipe? Obviously, all eggs vary slightly in size, but average, medium-sized eggs are the kind suggested for these recipes. However, if the available eggs are very small, use 3 small eggs for every 2 specified in the recipe. A reverse adjustment may be made if only very large (jumbo) eggs are available.

Sugar: White sugar should be sifted before use. Fine granulated sugar must be used, or the cake will have a somewhat coarse texture. Brown sugar, naturally lumpy and sticky, must be measured carefully. It should be packed into a measuring cup so firmly that it will hold together when removed.

Chocolate: Because chocolate has a low burning point, it should always be heated over indirect heat, never over direct heat. Do not add melted chocolate directly to other ingredients after removing it from the heat; allow it to cool for a minute or two.

HOW TO CHECK THE CAUSE OF CAKE FAILURE

Cake falls

1. Flour may be stale or incorrectly measured.
2. Cake did not bake long enough, or oven was opened before center was firmly set.
3. Oven temperature out of regulation.

Cake is flat and insufficiently risen

1. Pan used was too large for amount of batter.
2. Not enough leavening, or leavening was stale.
3. Wrong oven temperature.

Cake has a coarse-grained texture

1. All-purpose flour used; use cake flour.
2. Check carefully the measurements of all ingredients; possible error in proportions of ingredients used.
3. Excess leavening or too many egg yolks.
4. Oven temperature too low.
5. Ingredients not mixed together smoothly enough.
6. Sugar not fine enough.

Cake is too soft and falls apart

1. Excessive sugar, leavening, shortening; check measurements.
2. Not enough eggs, or stale eggs.
3. Oven temperature too low, or cake removed from pan before cooled.

Cake pulls away from sides of cakepan

1. Ingredients not at room temperature when combined. (This is particularly important for egg whites and liquids which should be at room temperature, not cold.)
2. Ingredients improperly mixed together.
3. Too much liquid used; check measurements of ingredients.
4. Oven temperature wrong; probably baked too long for temperature used.
5. Insufficient amount of batter for size of pan; measure size of pans.

Cake is too heavy

1. Excessive amounts of sugar, flour or fat; check amount specified against amount used.
2. Oven temperature wrong—probably too hot.
3. Too much mixing of batter; air bubbles may have broken down in overmixing.
4. If egg whites used, may not have been gently combined with other ingredients.

Cakes

Viennese Chocolate Layer Cake

1¾ cups sifted cake flour
1 teaspoon salt
2 teaspoons baking powder
1½ cups sugar
½ cup butter or margarine
1¼ cups light cream
2 eggs
1 teaspoon vanilla extract
2 squares (ounces) unsweetened chocolate, melted and cooled

Preheat oven to 350°. Grease two 9-inch layer cake pans and dust lightly with a little flour.

Sift together the flour, salt, baking powder and sugar. Cream the butter; sift in the flour mixture. Mix in 1 cup cream, then beat very well. Add the eggs, vanilla, chocolate and remaining cream. Beat very well again. Divide batter evenly between the two prepared pans. Bake 25 minutes or until a cake tester comes out clean. Cool on a cake rack 10 minutes before removing from pans. Cool thoroughly before frosting with rich Chocolate Frosting (see recipe).

Rich Chocolate Cake, Argentine Style

2½ cups sifted cake flour
½ teaspoon salt
1 teaspoon baking soda
¼ pound sweet chocolate
½ cup brewed coffee
1 cup (2 sticks) butter
1¾ cups sugar
4 egg yolks
1 cup buttermilk or sour milk
4 egg whites, stiffly beaten

Preheat oven to 350°. Grease three 8-inch layer cake pans and dust lightly with flour.

Sift together the flour, salt and baking soda. Combine the chocolate and coffee in the top of a double boiler; place over hot water until melted. Cool. Cream the butter; gradually beat in the sugar until light and fluffy. Add 1 egg yolk at a time, beating well after each addition. Mix in the melted chocolate. Add the flour mixture alternately with the buttermilk, beating until smooth after each addition. Fold in the egg whites. Divide batter evenly among the prepared pans. Bake 35 minutes or until a cake tester comes out clean. Cool on a cake rack 20 minutes before removing from pans. Cool thoroughly before frosting with Seven Minute Frosting, Cream Frosting or Whipped Cream.

Note: This cake is very rich and may crack and fall, but the flavor won't be affected.

Danish Chocolate Yeast Cake

2 envelopes yeast
¼ cup warm water
¾ cup milk, scalded and cooled
3 cups sifted flour
½ cup (1 stick) butter
2 cups sugar
3 eggs
1 package semi-sweet chocolate morsels, melted
1 teaspoon baking soda
½ teaspoon salt
½ teaspoon vanilla extract

Sprinkle the yeast into the water and stir until dissolved. Beat in the milk and 1½ cups flour until smooth. Cover and let rise in a warm place until light and spongy, about 30 minutes.

Meanwhile, cream together the butter and sugar. Add 1 egg at a time, beating well after each addition. Add yeast mixture, remaining flour, melted chocolate, baking soda, salt and vanilla. Beat until well-blended. Turn into a well-greased 10-inch tube pan. Cover and let rise in a warm place, free from draft, until light and bubbly, about 1 hour. Bake in a preheated 350° oven 50 minutes or until a cake tester inserted in center comes out clean. Cool on a cake rack 15 minutes, then turn out onto the rack. Let stand until cold. Serve with Coffee Whipped Cream, or split the cake into three layers and fill with the flavored whipped cream.

Upside-Down Chocolate Cake

1 cup sifted flour
¼ teaspoon salt
2 teaspoons baking powder
1¼ cups granulated sugar
7 tablespoons unsweetened cocoa
¾ cup milk
1 teaspoon vanilla extract
2 tablespoons melted butter or margarine
½ cup chopped walnuts or pecans
½ cup firmly packed brown sugar
1 cup water

Preheat oven to 350°. Grease an 8-inch square baking pan.

Sift the flour, salt, baking powder, ¾ cup granulated sugar and 2 tablespoons cocoa into a bowl. Mix in the milk and vanilla until smooth. Stir in the melted butter and nuts lightly. Spread evenly in the prepared pan. In a saucepan mix the brown sugar, water, remaining granulated sugar and cocoa. Bring to a boil, stirring until sugars dissolve. Pour over the batter in the pan. Bake 40 minutes or until a cake tester comes out clean. Cool on a cake rack 20 minutes, then turn out, bottom up. The fudge will now be on top. Cool and cut into 2-inch squares.

Chocolate Chiffon Cake

1¾ cups sifted cake flour
1 teaspoon baking soda
2½ teaspoons cream of tartar
2 cups sugar
⅔ cup unsweetened cocoa
½ cup vegetable oil
7 egg yolks
¾ cup cold water
1 teaspoon vanilla extract
1 cup egg white (9-10)
1 teaspoon salt

Preheat oven to 350°.

Sift together the flour, baking soda, 2 teaspoons cream of tartar, the sugar and cocoa into a large bowl. Make a well in the center and in it put the oil, egg yolks, water and vanilla. Beat until thoroughly blended.

Beat together the egg whites, salt and remaining cream of tartar until very stiff. Fold into the chocolate mixture carefully but thoroughly. Pour into a 10-inch tube pan. Bake 1 hour and 10 minutes or until a cake tester comes out clean. Invert and let cool in the pan (upside down) for 2 hours. (If tube pan doesn't have legs to keep top of cake away from a rack, place it on a saucer. Air must circulate.) Run a spatula around the edges and center tube, then turn out.

Fudge Cake

3 cups sifted cake flour
½ teaspoon salt
1½ teaspoons baking soda
5 eggs
4 squares (ounces) unsweetened chocolate
1¾ cups milk
2¼ cups sugar
¾ cup shortening
1½ teaspoons vanilla extract

Preheat oven to 350°. Grease three 9-inch layer cake pans and dust lightly with flour.

Sift together the flour, salt and baking soda. In a saucepan, beat 1 egg. Add the chocolate, broken into small pieces, ¾ cup milk and 1 cup sugar. Cook over low heat, stirring constantly, until chocolate melts. Cool.

Cream the shortening; gradually beat in the remaining sugar until light and fluffy. Add 1 of the remaining eggs at a time, beating after each addition. Add the flour mixture alternately with the remaining milk, beating well after each addition. Blend in the vanilla and chocolate mixture. Divide batter evenly among the prepared pans. Bake 30 minutes or until a cake tester comes out clean. Cool on a cake rack 20 minutes before removing from pans. Cool thoroughly before frosting.

Cheesecake with Sour Cream

1 cup graham cracker crumbs
½ cup ground almonds
¼ cup melted butter
1½ pounds cream cheese, at room temperature
1¼ cups sugar
1 teaspoon salt
¼ cup sifted flour
5 egg yolks
2 tablespoons lemon juice
1 teaspoon vanilla extract
½ teaspoon almond extract
1 cup sour cream
5 egg whites

Mix together the crumbs, nuts and melted butter. Pack onto the bottom of a greased 10-inch spring form. Chill 30 minutes.

Beat together the cheese, 1 cup sugar and the salt. Add the flour and 1 egg yolk at a time, beating until very smooth. Beat in the lemon juice, vanilla, almond extract and sour cream.

Beat the egg whites until soft peaks form, then gradually beat in the remaining sugar until stiff but not dry; fold into the cheese mixture. Slowly pour into the prepared chilled spring form. Bake in a preheated 325° oven 1¼ hours. Open the oven door, turn off the oven and leave cake to cool for 1 hour. Remove from oven and finish cooling on a cake rack, then chill before removing the sides of the pan.

Serves 10–12.

Coconut Cheesecake

1 pound cream cheese, at room temperature
¾ cup sugar
4 egg yolks
2 tablespoons flour
½ teaspoon salt
¼ cup fine-grated coconut
⅔ cup heavy cream
1 tablespoon cognac
4 egg whites
1 9-inch pastry or coconut shell

Preheat oven to 325°.

Beat the cream cheese until smooth, then beat in ½ cup sugar gradually. Add 1 egg yolk at a time, beating after each addition. Stir in the flour, salt and coconut, then the cream and cognac.

Beat the egg whites until stiff; gradually beat in the remaining ¼ cup sugar. Fold into the cheese mixture. Pour into the lined pie plate. Bake 45 minutes or until a knife inserted in the center comes out clean. Open the door, turn off the oven and let cake cool 1 hour. Remove from oven to finish cooling.

Refrigerator Cheesecake

18 zwieback, finely crushed
¼ pound (1 stick) butter, melted
¾ cup sugar
2 envelopes (tablespoons) gelatin
½ cup water
1 pound cream cheese
3 egg yolks
½ cup light cream
2 teaspoons grated lemon rind
1 tablespoon lemon juice
½ teaspoon salt
1 cup whipped cream
3 egg whites, stiffly beaten

Combine the zwieback, melted butter and ¼ cup sugar. Press on the bottom and sides of a 9-inch buttered spring form.

Soften the gelatin in the water for 5 minutes. Place over hot water and stir until dissolved.

Beat the remaining sugar and cheese; add the egg yolks, light cream, lemon rind, lemon juice, salt and gelatin. Beat until light and fluffy.

Fold the whipped cream into the cheese mixture. Fold the egg whites in carefully but thoroughly. Pour into the prepared spring form. Chill at least 4 hours.

Spice Sour Cream Cake

2 cups sifted flour
¼ teaspoon salt
1 teaspoon baking soda
2 teaspoons cinnamon
1 teaspoon ground allspice
½ teaspoon ground cloves
¼ pound (1 stick) butter
2 cups packed dark brown sugar
3 eggs
1 cup sour cream

Preheat oven to 350°. Grease two 9-inch layer cake pans. Sift together the flour, salt, baking soda, cinnamon, allspice and cloves. Cream the butter; gradually beat in the brown sugar until light and fluffy. Add 1 egg at a time, beating well after each addition. Add the sifted ingredients alternately with the sour cream, mixing only until blended. Turn into the pans. Bake 30 minutes or until a cake tester comes out clean. Cool on a cake rack 10 minutes, then turn out and cool completely before putting together with Butter Cream or whipped cream.

Italian Spice Nut Cake

(CERTOSINA)

1 cup sifted flour
¼ teaspoon salt
½ teaspoon baking soda
½ teaspoon ground cloves
½ teaspoon nutmeg
½ teaspoon cinnamon
½ cup sugar
½ cup honey
⅔ cup water
2½ cups blanched toasted sliced almonds
½ cup finely diced candied fruits

Preheat oven to 300°.

Sift together the flour, salt, baking soda, cloves, nutmeg and cinnamon.

Combine the sugar, honey and water in a saucepan. Cook over low heat, stirring constantly, until mixture boils. Remove from the heat and beat in the flour mixture until very smooth. Mix in the almonds and fruit. Turn into a well-oiled 9-inch pie plate. If you like, decorate the top with almonds and fruit. Bake 45 minutes or until a cake tester comes out clean. Cool thoroughly before turning out. Serve in very narrow strips.

Brazilian Nut Cake

10 egg yolks
1 teaspoon instant coffee
1¾ cups superfine sugar
3 cups ground nuts (walnuts, brazil, almonds)
⅛ teaspoon salt
2 tablespoons cognac
2 tablespoons bread crumbs
10 egg whites

Preheat oven to 350°.

Butter a 10-inch spring form and dust lightly with bread crumbs.

Beat the egg yolks and instant coffee; gradually add the sugar, beating until thick and light. Mix in the ground nuts, salt, cognac and the 2 tablespoons bread crumbs. Beat the egg whites until stiff but not dry; fold into the nut mixture. Turn into the prepared pan. Bake 50 minutes or until a cake tester comes out clean. Cool on a cake rack before removing the pan. Split and fill and cover with coffee-flavored whipped cream, if you like.

Brazilian Chocolate Nut Cake

2¾ cups sifted cake flour
½ teaspoon salt
2 teaspoons baking powder
¼ pound sweet chocolate
¼ cup brewed coffee
1 cup (2 sticks) butter
1½ cups sugar
4 egg yolks
1 teaspoon vanilla extract
¾ cup milk
1 cup finely chopped filberts, walnuts or pecans
4 egg whites

Preheat oven to 350°. Grease a 10-inch tube pan and dust lightly with flour.

Sift together the flour, salt and baking powder. Break the chocolate into small pieces and combine with the coffee in the top of a double boiler. Place over hot water until melted; cool.

Cream the butter. Gradually beat in the sugar until light and fluffy. Add 1 egg yolk at a time, beating well after each addition. Blend in the vanilla and melted chocolate. Add the flour mixture alternately with the milk, beating until smooth after each addition. Stir in the nuts. Beat the egg whites until stiff but not dry; fold into the chocolate mixture. Pour into the prepared pan; smooth the top with a spatula. Bake 1 hour or until a cake tester comes out clean. Cool on a cake rack 20 minutes before removing from pan. The cake may be served as is, cut in wedges, or split into as many layers as you like. Whipped cream or any filling may then be spread between the layers.

Sponge Cake

6 egg whites
1/8 teaspoon salt
1 1/8 cups fine granulated sugar
6 egg yolks
1 tablespoon lemon juice
1 teaspoon vanilla extract
1 teaspoon grated lemon rind
1 cup sifted flour

Preheat oven to 350°. Grease only the bottom of a 9-inch tube pan and dust it lightly with flour.

Beat the egg whites and salt until soft peaks form, then beat in 1 tablespoon of sugar at a time, beating steadily until stiff.

Beat the egg yolks until thick, then mix in the lemon juice, vanilla and rind. Fold about 1 cup of the egg whites into the yolks until no white remains. Pile the remaining egg whites on the yolk mixture, then sift flour over them. Fold together carefully. Turn into the pan and smooth top with a rubber spatula. Pick up pan carefully and hit bottom on a hard surface.

Bake 40 minutes or until top springs back when pressed with the finger and is browned. Cool on a cake rack.

Note: For layers, bake in two 9-inch layer cake pans for 25 minutes or until done.

Orange Sponge Cake

4 egg yolks
¾ cup sugar
⅓ cup orange juice
2 teaspoons grated orange rind
1¼ cups sifted cake flour
4 egg whites
⅛ teaspoon salt

Preheat oven to 350°. Place oven rack on middle level. Grease a 9-inch layer cake pan and dust lightly with flour.

Beat the egg yolks, then gradually add the sugar (reserving 2 tablespoons) beating with an electric mixer or wire whisk until thick and light. Beat in the orange juice and rind, then mix in the flour.

Beat the egg whites and salt until soft peaks are formed, then beat in the reserved sugar until stiff but not dry. Fold half the egg whites into the flour mixture then fold in the remaining egg whites lightly. Turn into the pan. Bake 30 minutes or until browned and slightly shrunk away from the sides of the pan. Cool in the pan 5 minutes, then run a spatula around the edge and turn out onto a cake rack. Turn right side up and let stand until cold. Sprinkle with powdered sugar or split, fill with Orange Cream Filling and glaze with Orange Glaze.

Almond-Cognac Sponge Cake

3 egg yolks
¾ cup sugar
⅓ cup cognac
¼ teaspoon almond extract
¾ cup ground blanched almonds
¾ cup sifted cake flour
¼ pound (1 stick) butter, melted and cooled
3 egg whites
⅛ teaspoon salt

Preheat oven to 350°. Place oven rack on middle level. Grease a 9-inch layer cake pan and dust lightly with flour.

Beat the egg yolks with an electric mixer or wire whisk; gradually add the sugar (reserving 2 tablespoons) beating until thick and light. Beat in the cognac and almond extract. Mix in the almonds and flour. Fold in the butter.

Beat the egg whites and salt until soft peaks are formed. Beat in the reserved sugar until stiff but not dry. Fold half the egg whites into the almond mixture, then fold in the remaining egg whites carefully. Turn into the prepared pan. Bake 30 minutes or until browned and top springs back when pressed with the finger. Cool in the pan 10 minutes, run a spatula around the edge and turn out onto a cake rack. Turn right side up and finish cooling. Sprinkle with powdered sugar or cover with Apricot Glaze.

Marquis Chocolate Sponge Cake

3½ squares (ounces) semi-sweet chocolate
2 tablespoons cognac or brewed coffee
4 tablespoons soft butter
3 egg yolks
½ cup plus 1 tablespoon sugar
⅔ cup sifted cake flour
3 egg whites
⅛ teaspoon salt

Preheat oven to 350°. Place oven rack on middle level of oven. Grease an 8-inch layer cake pan and dust lightly with flour.

Break the chocolate into small pieces and combine in a small saucepan with the cognac or coffee. Place over hot water and stir with a wooden spoon until melted and smooth. Remove from the heat and beat in the butter, a little at a time, until smooth.

Beat the egg yolks, then add ½ cup sugar, beating with an electric mixer or wire whisk until thick and light. Fold in the flour carefully.

Beat the egg whites and salt until soft peaks form, then beat in the 1 tablespoon sugar until stiff but not dry. Fold the chocolate mixture into the flour mixture. Fold in half the egg whites, then fold in the remaining egg whites carefully. Turn into the pan. Bake 30 minutes or until a cake tester comes out clean. (The top will crack in baking.) Cool in the pan 5 minutes, then run a spatula around the edge and turn out. Turn right side up and finish cooling on a cake rack. Sprinkle with powdered sugar, or split and fill with Butter Cream and cover with Chocolate Glaze.

Hot Milk Sponge Cake

1 cup sifted cake flour
¼ teaspoon salt
1 teaspoon baking powder
2 eggs
1 cup sugar
1 teaspoon vanilla extract
1 tablespoon butter
½ cup milk

Preheat oven to 350°. Grease only the bottom of an 8-inch square baking pan and dust lightly with flour.

Sift together the flour, salt and baking powder. Beat the eggs in a bowl until light and thick. Gradually beat in the sugar, then stir in the vanilla. Add the flour mixture gradually, stirring just until blended. Bring the butter and milk to a boil; add to the previous mixture, stirring steadily until smooth. Pour into the prepared pan. Bake 25 minutes or until a cake tester comes out clean. Cool on a cake rack.

Butter Sponge Cake

4 egg yolks
¾ cup sugar
2 teaspoons vanilla extract
1¼ cups sifted cake flour
4 egg whites
⅛ teaspoon salt
¼ cup melted butter, cooled

Preheat oven to 350°. Place oven rack in the middle level. Grease a 9-inch layer cake pan and dust lightly with flour.

Beat the egg yolks, then gradually add the sugar (reserving 2 tablespoons), beating with an electric mixer or wire whisk until thick and light. Beat in the vanilla. Carefully fold in the flour.

Beat the egg whites and salt until soft peaks form, then beat in the reserved sugar until stiff but not dry. Fold half the egg whites into the flour mixture, then fold in all the egg whites lightly. Fold in the melted butter. Turn into the pan. Bake 30 minutes or until browned and slightly shrunk away from the sides of the pan. Cool in the pan 5 minutes; run a spatula around the edge and turn out onto a cake rack. Turn right side up and let stand until cold. Sprinkle with powdered sugar, ice as you wish, or use for strawberry shortcake.

Sponge Cake

(WITH LEAVENING)

1⅓ cups sifted cake flour
½ teaspoon salt
½ teaspoon baking powder
1½ cups sifted very fine granulated sugar
6 egg yolks
¼ cup water
2 teaspoons lemon juice
6 egg whites
1 teaspoon cream of tartar

Preheat oven to 375°.

Sift together the flour, salt, baking powder and 1 cup sugar. Add the egg yolks, water and lemon juice. Beat just until smooth. Beat the egg whites and cream of tartar until soft peaks form, then beat in the remaining sugar gradually until very stiff. Fold in the egg yolk mixture carefully. Pour into an ungreased 10-inch spring form. Using a spoon or rubber spatula, cut through the batter to break up air pockets. Bake 35 minutes or until top springs back when pressed with the finger. Invert pan and let cool 2 hours. Run a spatula around the sides and center tube and turn out. Serve plain, or cut into layers and frost as you like.

Custard-Filled Sponge Roll

SPONGE ROLL

5 egg yolks
⅓ cup sugar
5 egg whites
⅓ cup sifted flour
⅛ teaspoon salt
½ teaspoon baking powder

Preheat the oven to 425°. Grease a jelly roll pan (11 by 17 inches), line with waxed paper and grease the paper.

Beat the egg yolks, gradually adding the sugar; continue beating until light and fluffy. Beat the egg whites until stiff but not dry; heap on the egg yolks, but don't mix. Sift the flour, salt, and baking powder over the whites; fold in carefully but thoroughly. Turn into the prepared pan; spread evenly. Bake 12 minutes. Carefully turn out onto a towel; peel the paper from the cake. Roll up the cake in the towel until cool.

CUSTARD FILLING

6 egg yolks
¾ cup sugar
½ cup sifted flour
2 teaspoons cornstarch
3 cups milk, scalded
2 teaspoons vanilla extract
Powdered sugar

In a saucepan, beat together the egg yolks, sugar, flour and cornstarch. Gradually add the hot milk, mixing steadily. Cook over low heat, mixing constantly, until thickened. Do not let boil. Remove from the heat and stir in the vanilla. Cool. Unroll the cake, spread filling on it, and roll up again. Sprinkle with powdered sugar. Cut into slices.

Serves 12–14.

Cake Roll

¾ cup sifted cake flour
¼ teaspoon salt
¾ teaspoon baking powder
4 eggs
¾ cup very fine granulated sugar
1 teaspoon vanilla extract
Confectioners' sugar

Preheat oven to 400°. Grease a jelly roll pan (15 by 10 by 1 inches). Line with waxed paper and grease again.

Sift together the flour, salt and baking powder. Beat the eggs until thick and light. Gradually beat in the sugar until thick and fluffy. Stir in the vanilla, then fold in the flour mixture. Spread the batter evenly in the prepared pan. Bake 12 minutes or until top springs back when pressed with the finger. Sprinkle a towel with confectioners' sugar and turn cake out onto it. Peel off the paper carefully and trim any crisp edges. Roll up the cake in the towel. Cool on a cake rack. Unroll and remove towel. Spread with desired filling and roll up again. Chill.

FILLING

Jelly or Jam: Spread cake with 1 cup jelly and 1 cup whipped cream.

Strawberry: Spread cake with 1 cup sweetened whipped cream and 1 cup sliced strawberries.

Chocolate: Spread cake with Chocolate Cream Filling.

Chocolate Roll

(BISCUIT ROULÉ AU CHOCOLAT)

6 ounces sweet chocolate
3 tablespoons brewed coffee
5 egg yolks
¾ cup sugar
1 tablespoon cognac
5 egg whites
Cocoa
1½ cups heavy cream, whipped
1 teaspoon vanilla extract

Preheat the oven to 350°. Grease a jelly roll pan (11 by 17 inches), line it with waxed paper and grease the paper.

Melt the chocolate in the coffee over low heat; cool. Beat the egg yolks, gradually beating in the sugar until thick and light. Mix in the chocolate and cognac. Beat the egg whites until stiff but not dry; thoroughly fold into the chocolate mixture. Turn into the prepared pan and spread evenly. Bake 15 minutes or until a cake tester comes out clean. Do not overbake. Cover the cake with a damp towel and place in the refrigerator for 1 hour.

Sprinkle a long piece of waxed paper with cocoa. Carefully turn out the cake and peel the paper from it. Mix the whipped cream with the vanilla and spread over the cake. Roll up the long way by gently raising the edge of the waxed paper. Don't worry if the roll cracks—patch it with a little more cocoa or cover with whipped cream.

Serves 10–12.

Colombian Cocoa Roll

2/3 cup sifted cake flour
1/4 teaspoon salt
3/4 teaspoon baking powder
1/3 cup unsweetened cocoa
1 cup very fine granulated sugar
6 eggs
1 teaspoon vanilla extract
Confectioners' sugar

Preheat oven to 350°. Grease a jelly roll pan (17 by 10 by 1 inch). Line with waxed paper and grease again.

Sift together the flour, salt, baking powder, cocoa and 1/4 cup sugar. Beat the eggs until thick and light. Beat in the remaining sugar gradually until very thick and smooth. Stir in the vanilla, then fold in the flour mixture a little at a time. Spread batter evenly in the prepared pan. Bake 18 minutes or until a cake tester comes out clean. Cool on a cake rack 3 minutes. Sprinkle a towel with confectioners' sugar and turn cake out on it. Carefully peel the paper from it and trim the edges if crisp. Roll up the cake in the towel. Continue cooling on a cake rack. Carefully unroll and remove the towel. Spread with Whipped Cream, Fluffy Chocolate Frosting, etc. and roll up again. Chill.

For a square thin layer cake, cool the cake on the towel, but don't roll up. Cut in 3 or 4 equal-sized pieces. Put together in layers with desired filling.

Nut Roll

6 egg yolks
¾ cup sugar
1½ cups ground nuts
1 teaspoon baking powder
1 teaspoon vanilla extract
6 egg whites
Confectioners' sugar
2 cups heavy cream
2 tablespoons cognac

Preheat the oven to 350°. Grease a jelly roll pan (11 by 17 inches); line it with waxed paper and grease the paper.

Beat the egg yolks and sugar together until thick and light. Toss the nuts with the baking powder and stir into the yolk mixture with the vanilla. Beat the egg whites until stiff but not dry. Fold into the nut mixture. Spread evenly on the prepared pan. Bake 15 minutes or until a cake tester comes out clean. Don't overbake.

Remove from the oven and cover with a damp towel until completely cool. Loosen from the pan. Sprinkle confectioners' sugar heavily on a piece of waxed paper. Turn out the cake and carefully peel the waxed paper from it. Whip the cream with 2 tablespoons confectioners' sugar. Stir in the cognac; spread on the cake and roll up lengthwise. The cake is very delicate, so don't worry if it cracks slightly in rolling. Cover outside with whipped cream, if desired.

Serves 8–10.

Gênoise

6 eggs
1 cup sugar
1 cup sifted flour
¼ pound (1 stick) sweet butter, melted and cooled
1 teaspoon vanilla extract

Preheat the oven to 350°. Grease two 9-inch layer cake pans and dust lightly with flour, or use a 9-inch tube pan.

Use an electric mixer if you have one, because this batter must be beaten a long time. Beat the eggs in a very large bowl, then beat in the sugar.

Place the bowl over, not in, a saucepan containing hot water. Beat until the egg mixture is almost tripled in volume. Scrape the bowl several times. Remove bowl from the saucepan and gently fold in the flour a little at a time. At the same time, fold in the butter and vanilla. Use a very light hand, or an electric mixer set at lowest speed, so as not to break the air cells. Turn into the pans or pan. Bake layers 25 minutes, tube pan 35 minutes, or until the top springs back when pressed with the finger. Invert onto a cake rack, remove pans and let cool.

VARIATIONS

Chocolate Gênoise: Use ½ cup sifted unsweetened cocoa and ½ cup sifted flour in place of all the flour. Sift together before adding. Proceed as directed.

Nut Gênoise: Add ½ cup ground nuts when adding the flour.

Tube Cake

3 cups sifted cake flour
1 teaspoon salt
2 teaspoons baking powder
1¾ cups very fine granulated sugar
1 cup (2 sticks) butter or margarine
½ cup milk
1 teaspoon almond extract
4 egg yolks
3 egg whites

Preheat oven to 375°. Grease a 9-inch tube pan and dust lightly with flour.

Sift together the flour, salt, baking powder and sugar. Cream the butter; sift the flour mixture over it, then pour milk and almond extract over all. Stir to dampen, then beat very well. Add the egg yolks and whites; beat again until very smooth. Turn into the prepared pan. Bake 50 minutes or until a cake tester comes out clean. Cool on a rack 20 minutes. Run a spatula around the sides and center, then turn out. Turn right side up and finish cooling on the rack. Sprinkle with confectioners' sugar or frost as you like.

Pineapple Upside-Down Cake

PINEAPPLE MIXTURE

1 8½-ounce can sliced pineapple
¼ cup melted butter
⅔ cup firmly packed brown sugar
½ cup flaked coconut

Preheat oven to 350°.

Drain the pineapple, reserving 2 tablespoons juice. Quarter the pineapple slices. Mix together the butter and sugar. Spread on the bottom of a 9-inch square baking pan. Sprinkle the reserved juice over it, then arrange the pineapple over it. Sprinkle with the coconut.

BATTER

2 cups sifted cake flour
¼ teaspoon salt
2 teaspoons baking powder
¼ cup shortening
1 cup sugar
1 egg
¾ cup milk
¾ teaspoon almond extract

Sift together the flour, salt, and baking powder. Cream the shortening; gradually beat in the sugar until light and fluffy. Add the egg; beat well. Add the flour mixture alternately with the milk, beating well after each addition. Mix in the almond extract. Turn into the prepared pan. Bake 45 minutes or until a cake tester comes out clean. Cool on a cake rack for 5 minutes. Invert on a serving dish and leave pan on cake for 2 minutes before removing. Serve warm, with whipped cream, if desired.

Serves 8–10.

Cocoa Layer Cake

2¼ cups sifted cake flour
1 teaspoon salt
1 teaspoon baking soda
½ cup unsweetened cocoa
1¾ cups sugar
1½ cups buttermilk or sour milk
½ cup shortening
2 eggs
1 teaspoon vanilla extract

Preheat oven to 350°. Grease two 9-inch layer cake pans and dust lightly with flour.

Sift together the flour, salt and baking soda. Mix the cocoa, ½ cup sugar, and ½ cup buttermilk until smooth. Cream the shortening; gradually beat in the remaining sugar until light and fluffy. Beat in 1 egg at a time. Add the flour mixture alternately with the remaining buttermilk, beating after each addition. Blend in the cocoa mixture and vanilla. Divide batter evenly between the prepared pans. Bake 30 minutes or until a cake tester comes out clean. Cool on a cake rack for 10 minutes before removing from pan. Cool thoroughly before frosting with Chocolate, Seven Minute or Mint Frosting.

Yellow Cake

2¾ cups sifted cake flour
1 teaspoon salt
1 tablespoon baking powder
1⅔ cups sugar
⅔ cup butter or margarine
1 cup milk
2 eggs
1 teaspoon vanilla extract

Preheat oven to 350°. Grease two 9-inch layer cake pans and dust lightly with flour.

Sift together the flour, salt, baking powder and sugar. Cream the butter; sift the dry ingredients into it, mixing lightly. Gradually add ¾ cup of the milk; beat 2 minutes with an electric mixer at low speed or with a wooden spoon for 4 minutes. Add the remaining milk, the eggs and vanilla. Beat 1 minute longer. Divide evenly between the pans. Bake 30 minutes or until a cake tester comes out clean. Cool on a cake rack for 10 minutes, then turn out onto the rack to cool completely. Frost as you like.

White Cake

2¾ cups sifted cake flour
¾ teaspoon salt
4 teaspoons baking powder
4 egg whites
1½ cups sifted fine granulated sugar
¾ cup shortening
1 cup milk
2 tablespoons heavy cream
1 teaspoon vanilla extract
½ teaspoon almond extract

Preheat oven to 350°. Grease two 9-inch layer cake pans and dust lightly with flour.

Sift together the flour, salt and baking powder. Beat the egg whites until foamy. Gradually beat in ½ cup sugar until soft peaks are formed. Cream the shortening; gradually beat in the remaining sugar until light and fluffy. Add the flour mixture alternately with the milk and cream, beating after each addition.

Stir in the vanilla and almond extracts, then mix in the beaten egg whites. Divide batter evenly between the prepared pans. Bake 30 minutes or until a cake tester comes out clean. Cool on a cake rack 10 minutes before removing from pans. Cool thoroughly before frosting as you like.

White Butter Cake

½ pound (2 sticks) butter
1⅔ cups sugar
2⅔ cups sifted flour
1 teaspoon vanilla extract
8 egg whites
⅛ teaspoon salt
¼ teaspoon cream of tartar

Preheat oven to 350°. Grease a 9-inch tube pan and dust lightly with flour.

Cream the butter; gradually beat in ⅔ cup sugar until light and fluffy. Beat in half the flour and all the vanilla.

Beat the egg whites, salt and cream of tartar until soft peaks are formed. Beat in the remaining sugar, 1 tablespoon at a time until very stiff. Fold half the egg whites into the butter mixture. Pile the remaining egg whites on top and sift the remaining flour over them. Fold together gently. Bake 50 minutes or until browned and cake shrinks away from the sides of the pan. Cool on a cake rack 30 minutes, then turn out to finish cooling on the rack.

Egg Yolk Cake

2¼ cups sifted cake flour
¾ teaspoon salt
2½ teaspoons baking powder
¼ pound (1 stick) butter or margarine
1 cup sugar
3 egg yolks
1 cup milk
1 teaspoon vanilla extract

Preheat oven to 375°. Grease two 8-inch layer cake pans and dust lightly with flour.

Sift together the flour, salt and baking powder. Cream the butter; gradually beat in the sugar until light and fluffy. Beat in 1 egg yolk at a time. Add the flour mixture alternately with the milk; beat well after each addition. Mix in the vanilla. Divide batter evenly between the prepared pans. Bake 25 minutes or until a cake tester comes out clean. Cool on a cake rack for 10 minutes before removing from pan. Cool thoroughly before frosting as you like.

Lemon Syrup Cake

1½ cups sifted cake flour
⅛ teaspoon salt
1 teaspoon baking soda
4 tablespoons butter
1¼ cups packed brown sugar
1 egg, beaten
¾ cup buttermilk or sour milk
¼ cup seedless raisins
2 teaspoons grated lemon rind
1 tablespoon rum
3 tablespoons lemon juice

Preheat oven to 350°.

Sift together the flour, salt and baking soda.

Cream the butter; gradually beat in 1 cup of the brown sugar until very light and fluffy. Beat in the egg. Add the flour mixture alternately with the buttermilk, beating after each addition. Mix in the raisins and lemon rind. Pour into a greased 8-inch square cake pan. Bake 30 minutes or until cake pulls away from the sides of the pan and is browned.

While the cake is baking, prepare the syrup. Bring the rum, lemon juice and remaining brown sugar to a boil. Mix until sugar dissolves. Cool.

Place cake on a cake rack and immediately pour the syrup over it. Serve warm or cold, cut into squares.

Raisin-Filled Cake

3 cups sifted flour
2 teaspoons cream of tartar
2 teaspoons baking soda
½ cup water
1 tablespoon cornstarch
⅞ cup sugar
1¼ cups seedless raisins
¾ cup chopped nuts
¾ cup (1½ sticks) butter
¾ cup dark brown sugar
3 eggs, beaten
¾ cup milk
1½ teaspoons vanilla extract

Preheat oven to 375°.

Sift together the flour, cream of tartar and baking soda.

In a saucepan, mix the water, cornstarch and ½ cup sugar. Cook over low heat, stirring constantly until thickened. Mix in the raisins and nuts. Cool while preparing the batter.

Cream the butter, gradually adding the brown sugar and the remaining white sugar. Beat in the eggs until light and fluffy. Add the dry ingredients to the butter mixture alternately with the milk. Stir in the vanilla. Pour half the batter into a buttered 8-inch square pan. Spread the raisin mixture over it and cover with the remaining batter. Bake for 35 minutes or until a cake tester comes out clean. Cool on a cake rack. Cut into 2-inch squares.

Raisin Tea Cake

1½ cups seedless raisins, white and dark
¼ cup cognac
½ pound (2 sticks) butter
1 cup sugar
6 egg yolks
1 teaspoon vanilla extract
6 egg whites
⅛ teaspoon salt
2 cups sifted flour

Preheat oven to 350°. Grease a 9-inch tube pan and dust lightly with flour.

Soak the raisins in the cognac 1 hour. Drain.

Cream the butter; gradually beat in ¼ cup sugar until light and fluffy. Beat in 1 egg yolk at a time. Mix in the vanilla and raisins.

Beat the egg whites and salt until soft peaks are formed, then beat in 1 tablespoon of the remaining sugar at a time. Continue beating until very stiff. Fold half the egg whites into the butter mixture. Pile the remaining egg whites over it, then sift the flour over them. Fold together carefully. Turn into the pan. Bake 50 minutes or until browned and cake shrinks away from the sides of the pan. Cool on a cake rack 20 minutes, then turn out and finish cooling on the rack.

Almond Tea Cake

¾ cup whole blanched almonds
4 whole eggs
4 egg yolks
1 cup sugar
1 teaspoon vanilla extract
2 tablespoons sifted cornstarch
1½ cups sifted flour
⅛ teaspoon nutmeg
½ pound (2 sticks) butter, melted and cooled

Preheat oven to 350°. Grease a 9-inch tube pan and dust lightly with flour. Arrange the almonds on the bottom of the pan.

In a large bowl, combine the eggs, egg yolks and sugar. Set the bowl over, not in, hot water and beat with an electric or rotary beater until almost tripled in bulk. Remove from heat. Stir in the vanilla gently. Sift the cornstarch, flour and nutmeg over the top and fold in gently, adding the butter gradually at the same time. Turn into the pan. Bake 50 minutes or until browned and cake shrinks away from the sides of the pan. Cool on a cake rack 20 minutes, then turn out to finish cooling.

VARIATION

Spanish Tea Cake: Grate 3 ounces semi-sweet chocolate and mix it with 1 teaspoon cinnamon. Pour one third the batter in the pan, sprinkle with one half the chocolate mixture, cover with half the remaining batter, sprinkle with remaining chocolate mixture and cover with remaining batter. Proceed as directed.

Dundee Cake

1¼ cups sifted flour
¼ teaspoon salt
½ teaspoon baking powder
½ cup currants
½ cup seedless raisins
¼ pound (1 stick) butter or margarine
⅓ cup sugar
2 eggs
¼ cup chopped blanched almonds
2 tablespoons orange juice
¼ cup chopped candied orange peel
¼ cup whole candied cherries
¼ cup whole blanched almonds

Preheat oven to 300°. Grease a 9-inch loaf pan; line it with heavy paper or aluminum foil and grease again.

Sift together the flour, salt and baking powder. Mix in the currants and raisins. Cream the butter; gradually add the sugar, beating until light and fluffy. Add 1 egg at a time, beating well after each addition. Mix in the chopped almonds; add the orange juice alternately with the flour mixture. Stir until well-blended. Mix in the orange peel. Turn into the prepared pan. Arrange the cherries and almonds on top. Bake 1¼ hours or until a cake tester comes out clean. Cover the top with a piece of aluminum foil when top begins to brown. Cool on a cake rack 15 minutes before removing from pan. Finish cooling on the cake rack.

English Seed Cake

2 cups sifted cake flour
¼ teaspoon cream of tartar
¼ teaspoon salt
½ pound sweet butter
1 cup sugar
4 eggs
1 egg yolk
¼ teaspoon mace
½ teaspoon vanilla extract
3 tablespoons caraway seeds

Preheat the oven to 350°. Line a greased 9-by-5-inch loaf pan with aluminum foil, and let the foil extend an inch or so along the top edge.

Sift together the flour, cream of tartar and salt. Cream the butter. Gradually beat in the sugar until very fluffy and light. Add 1 egg at a time, beating after each addition. Beat in the egg yolk, mace and vanilla. Fold in the flour mixture gradually until thoroughly blended, then fold in the caraway seeds. Turn into the lined pan. Bake 1¼ hours or until golden brown and a cake tester comes out clean. Cool in the pan on a cake rack for 10 minutes. Lift the cake out by the foil and finish cooling on the rack. Carefully peel the foil from the cake.

Orange Cake

3 cups sifted cake flour
½ teaspoon salt
1 tablespoon baking powder
¾ teaspoon baking soda
⅔ cup butter or margarine
1 tablespoon grated orange rind
1⅔ cups sugar
2 eggs
¼ cup milk
1 cup orange juice

Preheat oven to 375°. Grease two 9-inch layer cake pans and dust lightly with flour.

Sift together the flour, salt, baking powder and baking soda. Cream the butter, then mix in the orange rind. Gradually beat in the sugar until light and fluffy. Add 1 egg at a time, beating well after each addition. Add the flour mixture alternately with the milk and orange juice, beating until smooth after each addition. Divide batter evenly between the prepared pans. Bake 25 minutes or until a cake tester comes out clean. Cool on a cake rack 10 minutes before removing from pan. Cool thoroughly before frosting with Orange Butter Frosting.

Pound Cake

2 cups flour
1/8 teaspoon salt
1/2 pound soft butter
1 cup sugar
6 egg yolks
1 teaspoon vanilla extract or 1/2 teaspoon mace
6 egg whites

Preheat oven to 350°. Grease a 9-inch tube pan and dust lightly with flour.

Sift together the flour and salt. Cream the butter; beat in 1/2 cup sugar until very light and fluffy. Add 1 egg yolk at a time, beating well after each addition. Beat in the vanilla or mace.

Beat the egg whites until soft peaks form, then beat in 1 tablespoon at a time of the remaining sugar until very stiff. Pile the egg whites on top of the butter mixture, then sift the flour over the egg whites. Fold together carefully but thoroughly. Turn into the prepared pan. Bake 45 minutes or until browned and slightly shrunk away from the sides of pan. Cool on a cake rack 20 minutes, then run a spatula around the edges and turn out onto the rack. Pound cake should not be cut for several hours after it is baked.

Virginia Pound Cake

2 1/4 cups sifted cake flour
1/2 teaspoon salt
1 teaspoon baking powder
1 cup (2 sticks) butter
1 1/4 cups very fine granulated sugar
1/2 teaspoon mace
1 teaspoon vanilla extract
4 eggs
1/4 cup milk

Preheat oven to 325°. Grease a 9-inch loaf pan and dust lightly with flour.

Sift together the flour, salt and baking powder. Cream the butter until very fluffy. Very gradually beat in the sugar until extremely light. Mix in the mace and vanilla. Add 1 egg at a time, beating well after each addition. Add the flour mixture alternately with the milk, beating after each addition. Turn into the prepared pan. Bake 1¼ hours or until a cake tester comes out clean. Cool on a cake rack 20 minutes before removing from pan. Turn right side up to finish cooling. Bake the cake the day before it is to be served, if possible.

Light Fruit Cake

½ pound (2 sticks) butter
1 cup sugar
6 egg yolks
1 teaspoon vanilla extract
¼ teaspoon mace
2 cups flour
⅛ teaspoon salt
1½ cups mixed chopped candied fruit
½ cup coarsely chopped walnuts or pecans
½ teaspoon cream of tartar
6 egg whites

Preheat oven to 350°. Grease a 9-inch tube pan and dust lightly with flour.

Cream the butter and ¼ cup sugar until light and fluffy. Beat in 1 egg yolk at a time, then the vanilla and mace. Stir in 1¾ cups flour and the salt. Toss the fruit and nuts with the cream of tartar and remaining flour.

Beat the egg whites until soft peaks are formed, then beat in 1 tablespoon of the remaining sugar at a time until very soft. Fold half the egg whites into the butter mixture, then pile remaining egg whites over it. Sprinkle the fruit mixture on top, then fold all together gently. Turn into the pan. Bake 1 hour and 5 minutes or until browned and cake shrinks away from sides of pan. Cool on a cake rack before removing from pan.

Unbaked (Frozen) Fruitcake

¼ cup flour
¼ teaspoon salt
½ cup sugar
½ cup cold milk
1½ cups milk, scalded
2 eggs
¼ cup cognac
1 cup chopped pecans or walnuts
2 cups macaroon crumbs
1 cup chopped candied fruit
½ cup chopped candied cherries
1 cup heavy cream

Sift the flour, salt and sugar into a saucepan. Blend in the cold milk until smooth, then gradually stir in the scalded milk. Cook over low heat, stirring constantly, until mixture boils, then cook 5 minutes longer, stirring frequently.

Beat the eggs lightly in a bowl; gradually add the hot mixture, stirring steadily to prevent curdling. Return to saucepan; cook, stirring steadily, for 2 minutes, but do not let boil. Cool. Mix in the cognac, nuts, crumbs, fruit and cherries. Whip the cream lightly and fold into the fruit mixture. Turn into a buttered 9-by-5-inch loaf pan. Wrap carefully in aluminum foil. Freeze at least 24 hours before serving but cake will keep frozen one month. Let stand at room temperature 30 minutes before serving.

To serve, run a spatula around the edges. Turn out onto a serving dish. Decorate with nuts, cherries and whipped cream, if desired.

Serves 10–12.

Cupcakes

2 cups sifted flour
½ teaspoon salt
2 teaspoons baking powder
½ cup shortening
1¼ cups sugar
2 eggs
1 cup milk
1 teaspoon vanilla extract

Preheat oven to 375°. Line 24-muffin tins with paper cupcake liners, or grease and dust lightly with flour.

Sift together the flour, salt and baking powder. Cream the shortening; gradually beat in the sugar until light and fluffy. Beat in 1 egg at a time. Add the flour mixture and milk alternately, beating well after each addition. Stir in the vanilla. Spoon into the prepared pans. Bake 20 minutes or until a cake tester comes out clean. Cool on a cake rack. Frost as you like.

Devil's Food Cupcakes

1 cup sifted cake flour
½ teaspoon salt
½ teaspoon baking soda
¼ cup unsweetened cocoa
4 tablespoons (½ stick) butter
⅓ cup brown sugar
½ cup buttermilk or sour milk
½ teaspoon vanilla extract
2 egg yolks
1 egg white

Preheat oven to 350°. Line 18-muffin pans with paper cupcake liners, or grease and dust lightly with flour.

Sift together the flour, salt, baking soda and cocoa. Cream together the butter and brown sugar; mix in the flour mixture. Add half the buttermilk and the vanilla; beat well. Add the remaining buttermilk, the egg yolks and white; beat well again. Spoon into the prepared pans. Bake 25 minutes or until a cake tester comes out clean. Cool on a cake rack. Frost, if you like, with Chocolate or White Frosting.

Baba Au Rhum

1 cake or envelope yeast
1 tablespoon sugar
¼ cup lukewarm water
2 cups sifted flour
½ teaspoon salt
4 eggs, beaten
¼ cup light cream, scalded and cooled to lukewarm
⅔ cup soft butter
2 tablespoons currants or seedless raisins

Combine the yeast, sugar and water in a cup. Let stand 5 minutes. Sift the flour and salt into a bowl and make a well in the center. Pour in the eggs, yeast mixture and cream. Mix in the flour with the hand until a dough is formed. Pick up the dough and slap it down until smooth and elastic. Place in a bowl, cover with a towel and let rise in a warm place until double in bulk, about 1 hour. Punch the dough down and work in the butter and currants. Beat with the hand for 5 minutes. Transfer the dough to a fluted, buttered 7-inch ring mold. Cover and let rise in a warm place until double in bulk, about 1 hour. Preheat the oven to 450°.

Bake 10 minutes at 450°, then reduce the heat to 350° and bake 35 minutes longer or until browned and a cake tester comes out clean. Unmold onto a serving dish immediately and pour the Rum Syrup over it, which should be prepared while the Baba is baking.

SYRUP

1½ cups water
1 cup sugar
½ cup rum

Cook the water and sugar over high heat until thick and syrupy, about 5–7 minutes. Remove from the heat and stir in the rum. Pour over the Baba and let stand 3–4 hours. To serve aflame, sprinkle with 3 tablespoons confectioners' sugar and pour ¼ cup warm rum over it and set aflame.

Note: Small Babas can be made by spooning the dough into individual molds or muffin tins. Bake in a 375° oven for 20 minutes. Makes about 10. Babas can be served with ice cream, stewed fruits or whipped cream.

Savarin

1 envelope or package yeast
¼ cup lukewarm water
¼ cup milk, scalded and cooled
3 tablespoons sugar
½ teaspoon salt
2 cups sifted flour
4 eggs
⅔ cup butter, softened

Soften the yeast in the water, then stir in the milk, sugar, salt and ¾ cup of the flour. Work in the eggs and enough of the remaining flour to make a soft batter. Beat vigorously for a few minutes. Cover and let rise in a warm place for 45 minutes. Beat in the butter until smooth. Spread in a buttered 9-inch savarin or ring mold. Cover and let rise until double in bulk. Bake in a preheated 375° oven 45 minutes or until browned and shrunk away from the sides of the pan. Carefully turn out onto a serving dish and pour the syrup over it.

SYRUP

1½ cups strong tea
2 cups sugar
3 slices orange
3 slices lemon
¼ cup cognac or rum

Cook the tea, sugar, orange and lemon until syrupy. Discard fruit and add liquor. Spoon over the savarin until most of the syrup is absorbed. Fill the center with sweetened whipped cream.

Refrigerator Coffee Cake Dough

2 packages yeast
¼ cup luke warm water
¼ cup milk, scalded and cooled
¼ cup sugar
½ teaspoon salt
½ cup sour cream
1 teaspoon vanilla extract
2 egg yolks, beaten
3 cups flour (about)
¾ cup (1½ sticks) butter, softened

Stir the yeast into the water; let stand 5 minutes. Mix in the milk, sugar, salt, sour cream, vanilla and egg yolks. Add just enough flour to make a soft dough—it may not be necessary to use all the flour. Work in the butter. Knead on a lightly floured surface until very smooth and elastic. If too sticky, use a little more flour. Form into a ball, place in a bowl, cover and chill 4 hours or overnight. If chilled overnight, punch down twice. Use as directed in the following recipes.

SCHNECKEN

¾ cup packed brown sugar
½ cup chopped pecans or walnuts
½ cup seedless raisins
1 teaspoon cinnamon

Mix all the ingredients together. Divide dough into two pieces. Roll out each half into a rectangle ¼ inch thick. Sprinkle half the sugar mixture on each piece and roll up tightly like a jelly roll. Seal the edges with a little water or beaten egg. Cut in ½-inch slices. Arrange on a buttered baking sheet, leaving about 1 inch space between each. Cover with a towel and let rise until double in bulk, about 30 minutes.

Bake in a preheated 375° oven 20 minutes or until browned. Makes about 3 dozen.

COFFEE CAKE WREATH

Divide dough into three pieces. Roll each piece into a long strip, then braid the strips. Shape into a circle. Place on a buttered baking pan. Cover with a towel and let rise 30 minutes. Brush with melted butter. Bake in a preheated 375° oven 30 minutes or until browned.

Coffee Crumb Cake

2 cups sifted flour
1 teaspoon salt
½ cup sugar
2 teaspoons baking powder
1 egg, beaten
1 cup milk
⅓ cup vegetable oil

Preheat oven to 375°.

Mix and sift flour, salt, sugar, and baking powder into a bowl. Make a well in the center and into it put the egg, milk and oil. Stir only enough to dampen flour (batter should appear lumpy). Pour into a 10-inch pie plate. Sprinkle with the crumb topping. Bake 35 minutes or until brown.

TOPPING

Mix ¼ cup flour, ½ cup sugar and 1 teaspoon cinnamon in a bowl. Cut in 2 tablespoons butter with a pastry blender or 2 knives until the consistency of corn meal.

Tortes

Austrian Chocolate Torte

15 squares (ounces) semi-sweet chocolate
⅔ cup butter
4 egg yolks
1 teaspoon cinnamon
1 tablespoon sifted cornstarch
4 egg whites
3 tablespoons sugar

Preheat oven to 425°. Combine the chocolate and butter in the top of a double boiler; place over hot water until melted, stirring until smooth. Cool 10 minutes.

Beat the egg yolks until thick, then mix in the melted chocolate, cinnamon, sugar and cornstarch. Beat the egg whites until stiff but not dry; fold into the chocolate mixture. Turn into an ungreased, 8-inch spring form pan. Bake 20 minutes. Cool on a cake rack and remove sides of pan.

FROSTING

4 squares (ounces) semi-sweet chocolate
3 tablespoons light corn syrup
1½ teaspoons cognac
¼ cup sliced Brazil nuts or almonds

Combine the chocolate, syrup, and cognac in the top of a double boiler; place over hot water and stir until melted. Cool 10 minutes; then ice the torte. Sprinkle the nuts on top.

Serves 10–12.

Viennese Cocoa Torte

⅓ cup sifted unsweetened cocoa
1 cup ground almonds
6 eggs
⅔ cup sugar
1 teaspoon vanilla extract
⅓ cup melted butter, cooled
¼ cup cognac

Preheat oven to 350°. Grease only the bottom of a 9-inch tube pan.

Mix together the cocoa and nuts.

In a large bowl, beat the eggs and sugar. Set over, not in, a saucepan of hot water and beat with an electric or rotary beater until tripled in volume. Stir in the vanilla. Remove from the heat. Fold in the nut mixture and melted butter carefully. Turn into the pan. Bake 45 minutes, or until top springs back when pressed with the finger. Cool on a cake rack for several hours. Run a spatula around the edges and turn out. Sprinkle with the cognac. Cover with whipped cream or Chocolate Whipped Cream.

Apricot Meringue Torte

6 egg whites
1½ cups sugar
⅔ cup melted cooled butter
1½ cups sifted flour
1 pound apricot jam

Start preparing the torte the day before you want to serve it.

Preheat oven to 425°. Grease an 8-inch spring form and line it with waxed paper.

Beat the egg whites until peaks form; gradually add the sugar, beating until stiff but not dry. Fold in the butter and flour alternately, ending with the flour. Turn into the prepared pan. Bake 45 minutes; cool in the pan on a cake rack overnight.

Remove cake from pan and peel off the paper. Split cake into three or four layers and spread jam between them. Preheat oven to 350°.

MERINGUE

2 egg whites
½ cup sugar

Beat the egg whites until peaks form; add the sugar, gradually beating in until stiff but not dry. Spread over top and sides of cake. Place in oven and turn off the heat at once. Let stand in oven with door closed for 3 hours. Cool.

Serves 8–10.

Venezuelan Banana Torte

5 bananas
⅛ teaspoon salt
½ cup sugar
2 tablespoons butter
2 tablespoons lime or lemon juice
½ teaspoon nutmeg
1 cup whipped cream
1 8-inch baked pastry shell

Mash the bananas very smooth, or purée in an electric blender. Combine with the salt, sugar, and butter in a saucepan; bring to a boil. Cool, and fold in the lime or lemon juice, nutmeg and whipped cream. Turn into the pie shell. Chill.

Serves 6–8.

Viennese Poppy Seed Torte

1½ cups poppy seeds
6 egg whites
1 cup sugar
6 egg yolks
⅔ cup vegetable oil
1½ cups dry bread crumbs
2 teaspoons baking powder
¼ teaspoon salt
1 teaspoon vanilla

Place poppy seeds in a saucepan with enough water to cover; bring to a boil over medium heat and boil 30 minutes, adding more water if necessary. Drain thoroughly and cool. Beat egg whites until soft peaks form; gradually add ¼ cup of the sugar; continue beating until stiff but not dry.

Beat the egg yolks until thick and lemon-colored; gradually beat in the remaining sugar, then the oil. Mix in the poppy seeds. Mix together the bread crumbs, baking powder and salt. Blend into poppy seed–egg yolk mixture. Fold into the meringue mixture and add the vanilla. Turn into an ungreased 10-inch tube pan; bake in a preheated 325° oven for 1 hour. Invert over bottle or funnel to cool.

Italian Chestnut Torte

(TORTA DI CASTAGNA)

1½ pounds chestnuts
6 tablespoons butter
½ cup sugar
3 egg yolks
¾ cup sifted cake flour
2 teaspoons baking powder
¼ cup sliced almonds
2 tablespoons cognac
3 egg whites, stiffly beaten

Cut a crisscross in the pointed end of the chestnuts. Cover with water, bring to a boil and cook over low heat 40 minutes. Drain, cool slightly, peel and remove inner skin. Purée in an electric blender or force through a sieve. (You should have about 1 cup purée.) Preheat oven to 375°.

Cream the butter and sugar together until fluffy. Add I yolk at a time, beating after each addition. Beat in the chestnuts until smooth, then the flour, baking powder, almonds and cognac. Fold in the egg whites. Turn into two greased 8-inch layer cake pans. Bake 35 minutes, or until a cake tester comes out clean and cake shrinks away from sides of pan. Cool in the pans on a cake rack for 15 minutes, then turn out onto rack until completely cold. Fill and frost with the following recipe.

FROSTING

2 teaspoons instant coffee
1 tablespoon hot water
4 tablespoons butter
2 cups sifted confectioners' sugar
1 tablespoon cognac
2 tablespoons heavy cream

Dissolve the coffee in the water. Cream the butter, gradually adding the sugar. Beat in the coffee, cognac and cream.

Italian Chestnut Refrigerator Torte

(GATO DI CASTAGNA)

1 pound chestnuts
2 eggs
½ cup sugar
2 cups milk
1 square (ounce) unsweetened chocolate
3 tablespoons cognac
1 teaspoon vanilla extract
1 cup heavy cream

Cut a crisscross in the pointed end of the chestnuts. Cover with water, bring to a boil and cook over low heat 40 minutes. Drain, cool slightly, peel and remove inner skin. Purée in an electric blender or force through a sieve.

Beat the eggs and sugar in the top of a double boiler. Stir in the milk and the chocolate, broken into small pieces. Place over hot water and cook, stirring constantly until thickened. Remove from the heat. Beat in the chestnuts, 1 tablespoon cognac and the vanilla. Cool slightly, then turn into a well-greased 7-inch tube pan. Chill 4 hours or until firm. Carefully unmold onto a serving dish. Fill center with the cream, whipped and flavored with remaining cognac.

Serves 6–8.

Swiss Torte

3 egg whites
⅛ teaspoon salt
⅛ teaspoon cream of tartar
1 teaspoon vanilla extract
¾ cup fine granulated sugar
½ cup blanched ground nuts
¼ cup sifted cornstarch

Preheat oven to 325°. Grease and dust with flour the bottom of two 9-inch cake pans with removable bottoms, or grease and dust with flour an 11-by-18-inch baking pan and press a 9-inch round pan on the surface, to make two circles.

Beat the egg whites, salt, cream of tartar and vanilla until soft peaks form. Beat in 1 tablespoon of sugar at a time until ½ cup is used up and meringue is very stiff. Mix together the nuts, cornstarch and remaining sugar. Fold into the meringue. Divide batter between the two pans, or spread on the baking pan in the circles.

Bake 35 minutes or until dry to the touch. Cool. Put layers together with the following recipe.

FILLING

6 ounces semi-sweet chocolate
2 tablespoons strong coffee
¼ pound butter, softened
1 egg yolk
1 tablespoon cognac

Melt the chocolate in the coffee, stirring until smooth. Cool. Cream the butter until fluffy, then beat in the chocolate, egg yolk and cognac. Spread between the layers. Chill. This torte is especially good if made the day before it is to be served.

Austrian Filbert Torte

½ pound (1¾ cups) filberts (hazel nuts)
6 egg whites
⅛ teaspoon salt
¾ cup sugar
10 egg yolks
¼ cup cognac

Preheat oven to 350°. Grease the bottoms only of two 9-inch layer cake pans, line with waxed paper and grease paper. Grind the nuts very fine (in an electric blender or Mouli grater).

Beat the egg whites and salt until soft peaks form, then beat in 1 tablespoon sugar at a time until very stiff. Beat the egg yolks and 1 tablespoon cognac lightly. Fold about ¼ of the egg whites into the egg yolks. Pile the remaining egg whites over it and sprinkle the filberts on top. Fold together carefully but thoroughly. Divide between the lined pans.

Bake 30 minutes, or until delicately browned and top springs back when pressed with the finger. Cool on a cake rack 30 minutes. Carefully run a spatula around the edges and turn cakes out onto the rack. Peel the paper from the bottoms. Sprinkle with the remaining cognac. The torte may be put together and covered with Mocha Butter Cream or Coffee-Flavored Whipped Cream.

Austrian Linzer (Almond) Torte

1¼ cups sifted flour
½ teaspoon cinnamon
½ cup sugar
2 tablespoons unsweetened cocoa
⅓ pound (1 cup) shelled almonds
½ pound butter
2 egg yolks
2 hard-cooked egg yolks, sieved
1 teaspoon grated lemon rind
1 teaspoon vanilla extract
1½ cups raspberry jam
3 tablespoons heavy cream

Preheat oven to 350°.

Sift together the flour, cinnamon, sugar and cocoa. Grind the almonds very fine (use an electric blender or a Mouli grater). Mix into the sifted ingredients. Make a well in the center and into it put the butter, raw yolks, mashed cooked yolks, lemon rind and vanilla. Mix with the hand until a dough is formed. Chill 15 minutes.

Roll out two-thirds of the dough (between two sheets of waxed paper) to fit an 8-inch straight-sided cake pan. Spread with the jam. Roll out the remaining dough and cut into ¼-inch wide strips. Place over the jam in a lattice pattern. Brush the strips and edge with the cream. Chill 1 hour. Bake 45 minutes or until lightly browned. Cool.

Swiss Almond Torte

1¼ cups (2½ sticks) butter
1¼ cups sugar
1 egg
1¾ cups sifted flour
2¼ cups ground almonds
1 teaspoon almond extract
2 tablespoons heavy cream

Preheat oven to 325°.

Cream the butter and sugar together. Mix in the egg, then the flour, 2 cups almonds, and the almond extract until smooth. Turn into a buttered 9-inch spring form. Brush the top with the cream and sprinkle with the remaining almonds. Bake 50 minutes or until delicately browned and a cake tester comes out clean. Cool before removing from pan.

Serves 8–10.

Carrot Torte

¼ *cup dry bread crumbs*
12 *egg yolks*
¾ *cup sugar*
¼ *cup grated carrots*
¾ *cup ground almonds*
½ *cup grated apple*
1 *tablespoon cognac*
12 *egg whites*

Preheat the oven to 375°. Grease a 10-inch spring form and dust with the bread crumbs.

Beat the egg yolks; add the sugar, beating until light and fluffy. Stir in the carrots, almonds, apple and cognac.

Beat the egg whites until stiff but not dry; fold into the carrot mixture. Turn into the pan. Bake 45 minutes, or until a cake tester comes out clean. Cool before removing from pan. Cover with whipped cream.

Serves 10–12.

Italian Rum Torte

(ZUPPA INGLESE)

2 tablespoons cornstarch
¼ teaspoon salt
½ cup sugar
2 cups milk
3 egg yolks
1 teaspoon vanilla extract
36 lady fingers
1 cup rum
1 cup heavy cream
1 tablespoon confectioners' sugar

Sift the cornstarch, salt and sugar into a saucepan. Gradually beat in the milk, then the egg yolks. Cook over low heat, mixing steadily, until thickened and smooth, but don't boil the mixture. Remove from the heat and beat in the vanilla. Strain if there are any lumps. Cool.

Line the bottom of an 11-inch deep pie plate closely with some lady fingers; pour ¼ cup rum over it. Cover with half the cooled custard. Make another layer of lady fingers (reserving some for the top), sprinkle with ¼ cup rum, spread remaining custard over it and cover with remaining lady fingers. Sprinkle with ¼ cup rum. Cover and chill 3–4 hours. Just before serving, pour the remaining rum over the top, and cover with the cream whipped with the confectioners' sugar.

Cookies

Cream Cheese Cookies

1¾ cups sifted flour
½ teaspoon salt
½ teaspoon baking powder
1 3-ounce package cream cheese (at room temperature)
2 tablespoons sour cream
¼ pound (1 stick) butter
1 cup sugar
1 egg
1 teaspoon vanilla extract
3 tablespoons powdered sugar
2 teaspoons cinnamon

Sift together the flour, salt and baking powder. Beat the cream cheese and sour cream together until smooth and soft. Cream the butter; gradually beat in the sugar until light and fluffy. Mix in the egg and vanilla, then the cream cheese. Blend in the flour mixture. Shape into a ball, wrap in foil or waxed paper and chill overnight. Roll out the dough as thin as possible on a lightly floured surface. Cut into desired shapes with a floured cooky cutter. Arrange on greased baking sheets. Sprinkle with a mixture of the powdered sugar and cinnamon. Bake in a preheated 350° oven 12 minutes or until delicately browned. It is not necessary to bake all the dough at once. Keep in the refrigerator and bake as needed.

Makes about 5 dozen 3-inch cookies.

English Molasses Drop Cookies

1½ cups sifted cake flour
¼ teaspoon salt
¾ teaspoons baking soda
½ teaspoon cinnamon
¾ teaspoon ground ginger
¼ teaspoon nutmeg
¼ cup butter
½ cup sugar
1 egg yolk
¼ cup molasses
½ cup buttermilk

Sift together the flour, salt, baking soda, cinnamon, ginger and nutmeg. Cream the butter; gradually beat in the sugar until light and fluffy. Beat in the egg yolk then the molasses. Add the flour mixture alternately with the buttermilk, mixing well after each addition. Chill 1½ hours or until stiff enough to hold its shape. Drop by the teaspoon onto greased baking sheets, leaving 2 inches between each. Bake in a preheated 400° oven 10 minutes or until delicately browned. Remove from pans with a spatula.

Makes about 3 dozen cookies.

VARIATIONS

Molasses Raisin Cookies: Add ½ cup seedless raisins to the batter before chilling. Proceed as directed.

Molasses Nut Cookies: Add ½ cup coarsely chopped nuts to the batter before chilling. Proceed as directed.

Crisp Sugar Cookies

3½ cups sifted cake flour
½ teaspoon salt
2½ teaspoons baking powder
¾ cup (1½ sticks) butter
1½ cups sugar
2 eggs
1½ teaspoons vanilla extract
1 tablespoon milk

Sift together the flour, salt and baking powder. Cream the butter; gradually beat in the sugar until light and fluffy. Beat in 1 egg at a time. Add the flour mixture alternately with the vanilla mixed with the milk. Form into a ball, wrap in foil or waxed paper and chill 4 hours or overnight.

Roll out ⅛ inch thick on a lightly floured surface. Cut with a floured cooky cutter and sprinkle with sugar—cinnamon too, if you like. Arrange on ungreased cooky sheets. Bake in a preheated 400° oven 8 minutes or until delicately browned.

Makes about 6 dozen 3-inch cookies.

Vienna Sugar Cookies

(SABLÉ VIENNOIS)

1½ cups flour
2 teaspoons baking powder
¼ pound (1 stick) butter
1 cup sugar
3 egg yolks
1 teaspoon vanilla extract

Sift the flour and baking powder into a bowl. Make a well in the center and place the butter, sugar, egg yolks and vanilla in it. Using the hand, mix the ingredients in the well until smooth, then work in the flour. Chill for 2 hours.

Roll out to ¼-inch thickness. Cut with a floured cooky cutter and transfer to a baking sheet with a spatula. Bake in a preheated 375° oven 8 minutes or until lightly browned. Cool on a cake rack for 5 minutes before removing from pan.

Makes about 36 3-inch cookies.

Almond Cookies

1 cup sifted flour
1/8 teaspoon salt
1/3 cup sugar
1/2 cup ground blanched almonds
1/3 cup softened butter
1 egg
2 teaspoons grated lemon rind
3 tablespoons heavy cream
18 almonds, split

Sift the flour and salt into a bowl. Make a well in the center and into it put the sugar, almonds, butter, egg and lemon rind. Mix the ingredients in the well with a wooden spoon until smooth. With the hand, work in the flour. Form into a ball, wrap in foil or waxed paper and chill 2 hours. Roll out the dough 1/4 inch thick on a lightly floured surface. Cut with a floured cooky cutter. Arrange on a greased baking sheet. Brush with the cream and gently press a half almond in the center of each cooky. Bake in a preheated 350° oven 10 minutes or until delicately browned.

Makes about 24 3-inch cookies.

Crisp Butter Cookies

1 pound (4 sticks) butter
3/4 cup confectioners' sugar
1 egg yolk
2 tablespoons cognac
4 1/2 cups sifted flour (about)
1/2 cup very fine sugar

Cream the butter; gradually add the sugar, beating until light and fluffy. Beat in the egg yolk and cognac. Work in enough of the flour to make a fairly firm dough. Form into two balls, wrap in foil or waxed paper and chill 3 hours.

Remove one ball at a time and roll 1/3 inch thick between two sheets of waxed paper. Cut into any shape you like with a floured cooky cutter. Work quickly, as dough becomes soft at room temperature. Arrange on ungreased cooky sheets. Bake in a preheated 350° oven 15 minutes or until edges begin to brown. Cool on a cake rack 10 minutes, then sprinkle with the fine sugar.

Makes about 4 dozen 3-inch cookies.

Oatmeal Cookies

¾ cup sifted flour
½ teaspoon salt
½ teaspoon baking soda
¼ pound (1 stick) butter
½ cup granulated sugar
½ cup packed brown sugar
1 egg, beaten
1½ cups quick-cooking rolled oats, uncooked
1 teaspoon vanilla extract

Sift together the flour, salt and baking soda. Cream the butter; gradually beat in the granulated and brown sugars until light and fluffy. Beat in the egg. Mix in the flour mixture, then the oats and vanilla. Shape into rolls 2 inches thick. Wrap in foil or waxed paper; chill until firm.

With a sharp knife, cut the rolls in ⅛-inch slices. Arrange on greased baking sheets leaving 1 inch between each. Bake in a preheated 400° oven 10 minutes. Cool on a cake rack.

Makes about 3 dozen cookies.

Jam Cookies

½ pound (2 sticks) butter, at room temperature
½ teaspoon salt
1¾ cups thinly slivered blanched almonds
2½ cups sifted flour
½ cup heavy cream
Sugar
1½ cups raspberry jam

Cream the butter, then blend in the salt and almonds. Add the flour alternately with the cream. Form into two balls, wrap in foil or waxed paper and chill 1 hour.

Heavily sprinkle a pastry cloth, piece of waxed paper or a board with sugar and roll out each piece of dough very thin. Cut into circles with a 1 or 2-inch round, floured cooky cutter. Using a smaller cutter or shot glass, cut out the centers of half the circles. Transfer cookies to greased cooky sheets with a spatula. Bake in a preheated 350° oven (with oven rack on middle level) 8 minutes or until delicately browned. Transfer cookies to a cake rack with a spatula and cool. Spread solid cookies with jam and cover with the cut-out cooky. Fill centers with a little more jam.

Makes about 20 2-inch cookies.

Swedish Honey Cookies

2 cups sifted flour
½ teaspoon salt
½ teaspoon baking soda
¾ teaspoon ginger
½ teaspoon cinnamon
½ teaspoon nutmeg
¼ pound (1 stick) butter
⅓ cup brown sugar
⅔ cup honey

Grease two or three cooky sheets and dust lightly with flour.

Sift together the flour, salt, baking soda, ginger, cinnamon and nutmeg. Cream the butter and sugar together until light and fluffy. Beat in the honey, then work in the flour mixture until a soft dough is formed. Divide in two and wrap in foil or waxed paper; chill 1 hour or until firm enough to roll.

Roll out each piece as thin as possible on a well-floured surface. Cut into any shape or shapes you like. Transfer to the pans with a spatula. Bake in a preheated 350° oven (with oven rack on middle level) 8 minutes or until delicately browned and puffed. Cool on a cake rack.

Makes about 4 dozen.

Meringue Coconut Cookies

- *1 cup (6-ounce package) semi-sweet chocolate chips*
- *2 egg whites*
- *1/8 teaspoon salt*
- *1/2 cup very fine granulated sugar*
- *1/2 teaspoon vinegar*
- *3/4 teaspoon vanilla extract*
- *1/2 cup fine grated coconut*
- *1/4 cup chopped pecans or walnuts*

Preheat oven to 350°. Grease two baking sheets.

Melt the chocolate over hot water; cool. Beat the egg whites and salt until foamy. Add 1 tablespoon sugar at a time, beating after each addition. Beat until stiff, then beat in the vinegar and vanilla. Fold in the chocolate, coconut and nuts. Drop by the teaspoon onto the pans, 1 inch apart. Bake 10 minutes. Remove from pans with a spatula.

Makes about 3 dozen.

Greek Pistachio Cookies

½ pound softened sweet butter
6 tablespoons sifted confectioners' sugar
1 egg yolk
2 teaspoons ouzo *(a Greek liquor) or cognac*
2¼ cups sifted cake flour
Pistachio nuts

Cream the butter until very soft and fluffy. Beat in the confectioners' sugar, then the egg yolk and *ouzo* or cognac. Work in the flour until a dough is formed. Chill 1 hour.

Break off pieces of the dough and form into balls about 1 inch in diameter. Arrange on cooky sheets and press a pistachio nut into each. Bake in a preheated oven 15 minutes or until pale gold in color. Cool, and sprinkle with confectioners' sugar.

Makes about 3 dozen.

Walnut Slices

1¾ cups sifted flour
⅛ teaspoon salt
½ teaspoon baking soda
¼ pound (1 stick) butter
1 cup packed dark brown sugar
1 egg
½ teaspoon vanilla extract
½ cup ground walnuts

Sift together the flour, salt and baking soda.

Cream the butter, then beat in the brown sugar until fluffy. Mix in the egg and vanilla until smooth and fluffy. Add flour mixture to the butter mixture. Work in the nuts. The dough should be very stiff. Form into two rolls 1 inch in diameter. Wrap in foil or waxed paper and chill for 2 hours.

Slice the rolls very thin and arrange on a cooky sheet. Bake on the middle level of a preheated 375° oven 10 minutes.

Makes about 3 dozen.

Spanish Almond Delights

½ pound (2 sticks) butter
1 cup sugar
3 eggs
2 tablespoons grated lemon rind
2 tablespoons cognac
¼ teaspoon almond extract
1 cup sifted flour
2 cups ground bleached almonds
4 tablespoons heavy cream
¾ cup slivered almonds

Cream the butter, gradually adding the sugar. Beat until fluffy. Add 1 egg at a time, beating well after each addition. Mix in the lemon rind, cognac, almond extract, flour, and ground almonds. Form into a ball; wrap in waxed paper and chill 3 hours.

Roll out the dough as thin as possible on a lightly floured surface. Cut with a floured cooky cutter into any shapes desired. Transfer with a spatula to a buttered baking sheet. Brush with the cream and sprinkle with the slivered almonds. Bake in a preheated 375° oven for 12 minutes or until delicately browned.

Makes about 4 dozen 3-inch cookies.

Barcelona Almond Drops

(ROSCAS ALMENDRA)

3 egg whites
4 tablespoons sugar
2 tablespoons grated lemon rind
2 cups ground blanched almonds

Preheat oven to 350°.

Beat the egg whites until stiff but not dry. Beat in the sugar gradually, then fold in the rind and almonds. Put through a pastry bag in small twists or drop by the teaspoon onto a greased baking sheet. Bake 10 minutes or until delicately browned.

Makes about 3 dozen.

Almond Meringue Strips

BATTER

4 egg yolks
1 egg white
1 cup sugar
1 cup ground toasted almonds
2 teaspoons grated lemon rind

Preheat oven to 275°. Grease an 8-inch square baking pan and dust with flour.

Beat the egg yolks until thick. Beat the egg whites until peaks form; then gradually beat in the sugar until stiff. Fold into the yolks with the almonds and lemon rind. Turn into the pan. Bake 25 minutes or until firm when pressed with the fingers. Cool, then turn out onto a baking sheet. Cover with the following meringue.

MERINGUE

¼ cup water
¾ cup sugar
3 egg whites

Boil the water and sugar until a thread forms when a fork is lifted from the syrup. Beat the egg whites until stiff, then gradually beat in the syrup. Cover the top and sides of the cake, and place in a 275° oven for 10 minutes or until delicately browned. Cool and cut in strips.

Viennese Almond Crescents

¾ cup sifted flour
⅛ teaspoon salt
¼ pound sweet butter
⅔ cup sugar
4 hard-cooked egg yolks, finely mashed
2 teaspoons grated orange or lemon rind
3 tablespoons heavy cream
¼ cup ground almonds

Sift the flour and salt into a bowl. Blend in the butter with the hand, then ½ cup sugar, the egg yolks and rind, mixing lightly until a ball of dough is formed. Chill 2 hours. Preheat the oven to 400°.

Break off small pieces of dough and roll on a lightly floured surface into 2-inch pencil-slim strips. Work quickly to keep dough from melting. Arrange on a cooky sheet and turn ends toward each other to form a crescent. Brush with the cream and sprinkle with the nuts mixed with the remaining sugar. Chill 30 minutes. Bake 10 minutes or until delicately browned. Cool on a cake rack.

Nut Slices

2 cups sifted flour
⅛ teaspoon salt
1½ teaspoons baking powder
¼ pound (1 stick) butter or margarine
¾ cup granulated sugar
½ cup firmly packed brown sugar
1 egg yolk, beaten
1 tablespoon milk
1½ teaspoons vanilla extract
1 cup chopped nuts

Sift together the flour, salt and baking powder. Cream the butter; beat in the granulated and brown sugars until light and fluffy. Mix in the egg yolk, milk and vanilla, then the nuts. Shape into rolls 1½ inches thick; wrap in aluminum foil or waxed paper. Chill overnight.

With a sharp knife, cut the rolls into slices ⅛ inch thick. Arrange on ungreased baking sheets. Bake in a preheated 400° oven 5 minutes or until delicately browned. The dough can be refrigerated for 2 weeks, so don't bake them all at once if you don't need that many.

Makes about 8 dozen cookies.

Crisp Chocolate Nut Cookies

½ pound semi-sweet chocolate
1 tablespoon brewed coffee
8 egg yolks
⅛ teaspoon salt
½ cup sugar
1 teaspoon vanilla extract
1⅓ cups ground blanched almonds
¾ cup flour

Preheat oven to 350°. Grease a cooky sheet and dust lightly with flour.

Break the chocolate into small pieces and combine with the coffee in a saucepan. Place over hot water until melted and smooth. Cool.

Beat the egg yolks, salt and sugar until thick and light. Mix in the vanilla, then the chocolate, nuts and flour. Put through a pastry bag with round tube or drop by the teaspoon onto the cooky sheet, 1 inch apart. Bake 25 minutes or until firm. Cool on a cake rack, and remove with a spatula.

Makes about 3 dozen.

Austrian Nut Crescents

¼ pound (1 stick) butter
6 tablespoons granulated sugar
¾ cup ground walnuts
1⅛ cups sifted flour (about)
Confectioners' sugar

Cream the butter; gradually add the granulated sugar, beating until light and fluffy. Mix in the nuts, then work in just enough of the flour to make a fairly firm dough. Form into a ball, wrap in foil or waxed paper and chill 2 hours.

Break off pieces of the dough and roll it between the palms of the hand into rolls 2 inches long and ½ inch in diameter. Turn ends toward each other to form a crescent, and arrange on ungreased cooky sheets. Bake in a preheated 350° oven 15 minutes or until browned around the edges. Cool on a cake rack 10 minutes, then sift confectioners' sugar over them.

Makes about 3 dozen.

Chocolate Nut Drop Cookies

2 squares (ounces) unsweetened chocolate
1½ cups sifted cake flour
½ teaspoon salt
½ teaspoon baking soda
¼ pound (1 stick) butter
1 cup firmly packed brown sugar
1 egg, beaten
½ cup milk
1 teaspoon vanilla extract
½ cup chopped walnuts or pecans
Mocha Glaze
36 walnut or pecan halves

Preheat oven to 350°. Grease two baking sheets.

Break the chocolate into small pieces; melt over hot water. Cool while preparing the batter. Sift together the flour, salt and baking soda. Cream the butter; gradually beat in the brown sugar until light and fluffy. Mix in the egg and chocolate until smooth. Add the flour mixture alternately with the milk and vanilla, mixing well after each addition. Mix in the chopped nuts. Drop by the heaping teaspoon onto the pans, 2 inches apart. Bake 10 minutes. While still warm, spread with the Mocha Glaze, and place a nut half in the center of each.

Makes about 3 dozen cookies.

Macaroons

Israeli Almond Macaroons

1 cup (4½ ounces) ground unblanched almonds
¾ cup sugar
1 tablespoon flour
¼ teaspoon salt
2–3 egg whites
¼ teaspoon almond extract
24 blanched almond halves

Preheat oven to 300°. Cover two baking sheets with brown paper or any unglazed paper.

With the hand, mix together the almonds, sugar, flour and salt until thoroughly blended. Beat in 1 egg white at a time until mixture has the consistency of soft mashed potatoes. It may not be necessary to use the third egg white. Mix in the extract. Force the mixture through a pastry tube or drop by the teaspoonful, leaving two inches between each. Press an almond half into each.

Bake on the lowest rack 25 minutes or until very delicately browned. Place the papers (macarooms will adhere to them) on a cake rack upside down, and place a damp towel on the paper for 5 minutes. Carefully peel the paper from the macaroons. Cool completely, then keep in an air-tight container.

Makes about 24.

Coconut Macaroons

¾ cup sweetened condensed milk
⅛ teaspoon salt
2 cups (7-ounce package) fine-grated coconut
1 teaspoon almond extract

Preheat oven to 325°.

Mix all the ingredients together until well-blended. Drop by the teaspoon onto a wet baking sheet, leaving 1 inch between each. Bake 15 minutes or until delicately browned. Remove from pan immediately with a spatula.

Makes about 30.

VARIATION

Chocolate-Almond Macaroons: Add 2 tablespoons unsweetened cocoa, ½ cup chopped almonds, 2 tablespoons melted butter and an additional 2 tablespoons condensed milk to the coconut macaroon mixture. Proceed as directed.

Makes about 36.

Florentines

4 tablespoons butter
¼ cup sugar
¼ cup chopped candied orange peel
½ cup blanched almonds, chopped fine
⅓ cup sifted flour
3 tablespoons heavy cream

Preheat oven to 375°.

Cream the butter, then beat in the sugar until light and fluffy. Mix in the orange peel, nuts and flour. Stir in the cream. Drop scant teaspoons of the mixture onto buttered cooky sheets, leaving 2 inches between each. Flatten with a wet fork. Bake 8 minutes or until browned. Cool 5 minutes, then remove from pan with a spatula.

Makes about 24.

Spanish Crisps

¾ cup (1½ sticks) butter
⅓ cup sugar
1½ teaspoons cinnamon
3 egg yolks
1½ cups sifted flour
3 tablespoons heavy cream
¼ cup confectioners' sugar

Preheat oven to 350°.

Cream the butter, sugar and cinnamon together. Work in the egg yolks and then the flour until smooth. Chill 30 minutes. Roll out ¼ inch thick and cut into half-moons. Arrange on a cooky sheet; brush with the cream and sprinkle with the confectioners' sugar. Bake 10 minutes or until browned.

Makes about 4 dozen.

Gingersnaps

2¼ cups sifted flour
¾ teaspoon salt
¾ teaspoon baking soda
¼ cup sugar
1½ teaspoons cinnamon
1½ teaspoons ground ginger
⅔ cup shortening
1 cup molasses
2 teaspoons cider vinegar

Sift together the flour, salt, baking soda, sugar, cinnamon and ginger. Blend in the shortening until mixture is like coarse corn meal. Bring the molasses and vinegar to a boil, then stir it into the flour mixture until a dough is formed. Shape into 2 balls and wrap in foil or waxed paper. Chill overnight or for at least 4 hours. Roll out each ball as thin as possible on a lightly floured surface. Cut into any shape you like with a floured cooky cutter. Arrange on lightly greased baking sheets. Bake in a preheated 400° oven 6 minutes or until edges are delicately browned. Remove from pan immediately with a spatula and let cool on a cake rack.

Makes about 4 dozen 3-inch cookies.

Ladyfingers

½ cup sifted cake flour
⅛ teaspoon salt
3 egg whites
⅓ cup sifted very fine granulated sugar
3 egg yolks
1 tablespoon hot water
1 teaspoon vanilla extract

Preheat oven to 350°. Line a cooky sheet with paper.

Sift the flour and salt 3 times. Beat the egg whites until soft peaks form, then gradually (1 tablespoon at a time) beat in the sugar until very stiff. Beat the egg yolks until thick and light; fold into the egg whites with the water and vanilla. Fold in the flour. Put through a plain-tubed pastry bag onto the paper in 2½-inch lengths, or form into finger lengths with a spoon, leaving ½ inch space between each. Bake 10 minutes or until delicately browned. Cool 2 minutes, then remove from the paper. If they stick, dampen the underside of the paper. Finish cooling. Make sandwiches of the fingers; brush half the fingers with lightly beaten egg white or jelly and cover with the remaining fingers.

Makes about 24.

Fudge Brownies

2 squares (ounces) unsweetened chocolate
¾ cup sifted flour
½ teaspoon salt
1 cup coarsely chopped walnuts
⅓ cup butter
1 cup sugar
2 eggs
¾ teaspoon vanilla extract

Preheat oven to 350°. Grease an 8-inch square pan.

Melt the chocolate over hot water. Cool. Sift together the flour and salt; stir in the nuts. Cream the butter; gradually beat in the sugar until light and fluffy. Add 1 egg at a time, beating well after each addition. Mix in the vanilla and chocolate. Stir in the flour mixture until well-blended. Turn into the prepared pan. Bake 30 minutes or until a cake tester comes out clean. Cool on a cake rack and cut into 2-inch squares. These brownies are very moist and fall slightly when removed from oven. For crisper brownies, add ½ teaspoon baking powder to flour mixture.

VARIATION

Peppermint Brownies: When brownies are baked, arrange 16 chocolate-covered peppermints on top; return to oven for 3 minutes. Remove from oven and smooth melted peppermints over the top.

Butterscotch Brownies

1 cup sifted flour
½ teaspoon salt
½ teaspoon baking powder
⅛ teaspoon baking soda
¾ cup coarsely chopped walnuts or pecans
⅓ cup butter or margarine
1 cup firmly packed dark brown sugar
1 tablespoon hot water
1 egg
1 teaspoon vanilla extract
½ cup caramel or chocolate chips

Preheat oven to 350°. Grease an 8-inch square baking pan.

Sift together the flour, salt, baking powder and baking soda. Stir in the nuts. Melt the butter in a saucepan. Remove from heat; mix in the brown sugar and water until dissolved. Cool. Beat in the egg and vanilla. Gradually stir in the flour mixture until smooth. Pour into the prepared pan. Sprinkle the caramel chips on top. Bake 20 minutes or until a cake tester comes out clean. Cool on a cake rack. Cut into 2-inch squares.

Butterscotch Squares

2 cups sifted cake flour
1 teaspoon salt
½ teaspoon baking soda
½ cup butter
1⅓ cups packed brown sugar
¾ cup milk
1½ teaspoons vanilla extract
2 eggs

Preheat oven to 375°. Grease a 9-inch square pan and dust lightly with flour.

Sift together the flour, salt and baking soda. Cream the butter; sift in the flour mixture. Beat in the brown sugar; add the milk and vanilla, beating very well. Beat in the eggs for 1 minute. Pour into the prepared pan. Bake 35 minutes or until a cake tester comes out clean. Cool on a cake rack for 10 minutes. Turn out and cool completely before frosting with Caramel Frosting. Cut into squares.

Coconut Pecan Squares

1¼ cups sifted cake flour
⅛ teaspoon salt
1¼ cups firmly packed brown sugar
⅓ cup melted butter
2 eggs
½ teaspoon double-acting baking powder
½ teaspoon almond extract
1¼ cups flaked coconut
1 cup chopped pecans

Preheat oven to 350°.

In a bowl, mix 1 cup flour, the salt and ¼ cup brown sugar. Mix in the butter until smooth. Press on the bottom of an 8-inch square baking pan. Bake 15 minutes.

Prepare the topping during this time. Beat the eggs until thick; gradually beat in the remaining brown sugar until light and fluffy. Sift the baking powder and remaining flour into the mixture; stir until smooth. Mix in the almond extract, coconut and nuts. Remove pan from oven and quickly spread coconut mixture over the pastry. Return to oven and bake 20 minutes longer or until delicately browned. Cut into 2-inch squares while warm.

Chocolate Balls

3 squares (ounces) unsweetened chocolate
1 tablespoon brewed coffee
½ pound (2 sticks) butter
¼ cup sugar
1 egg yolk
1 cup ground walnuts or or pecans
1 tablespoon rum
2½ cups sifted flour
Sugar for rolling
Walnut or pecan halves

Break the chocolate into small pieces and combine with the coffee in a small saucepan. Place over hot water until melted and smooth. Cool.

Cream the butter and sugar until light and fluffy. Beat in the egg yolk, nuts, rum and chocolate, then mix in the flour. Chill 1 hour.

Form teaspoons of the dough into balls, roll in sugar and arrange on greased cooky sheets, leaving space between each. Lightly press a nut half into each ball. Bake in a preheated 325° oven 15 minutes or until dry. Cool on a cake rack.

Makes about 4 dozen.

Chocolate Date-Nut Bars

1 cup finely chopped dates
1 cup boiling water
1 teaspoon baking soda
1¾ cups sifted flour
¼ cup unsweetened cocoa
½ teaspoon salt
1 cup shortening
1 cup sugar
2 eggs
1 teaspoon vanilla extract
1 cup semi-sweet chocolate chips
½ cup chopped pecans or walnuts

Preheat oven to 350°. Grease a 10-by-15-inch jelly roll pan. Combine the dates, boiling water and baking soda. Let stand until cool. Sift together the flour, cocoa and salt.

Cream the shortening. Gradually beat in the sugar until light and fluffy. Beat in 1 egg at a time, then the vanilla. Add the flour mixture alternately with the date mixture, beating well after each addition. Spread in the prepared pan. Arrange the chocolate chips and nuts over it. Bake 30 minutes. Cool on a cake rack; cut into 36 bars while still warm.

Polish Almond Bars

(MAZURKA)

½ pound (2 sticks) butter
1 cup sugar
5 hard-cooked egg yolks, mashed
½ teaspoon vanilla extract
⅛ teaspoon salt
2¼ cups sifted flour
1 egg white
1 teaspoon water
1½ cups sliced blanched almonds

Grease an 8-inch square shallow baking pan. Place oven rack on middle level.

Cream the butter and sugar together until light and fluffy. Blend in the mashed egg yolks, vanilla and salt. Stir in the flour until smooth. Pat the dough into the pan. Chill 2 hours.

Brush the top of the dough with the egg white mixed with the water. Sprinkle the almonds over it. Bake in a preheated 350° oven 40 minutes or until delicately browned and firm. Cool 5 minutes, then with a sharp knife cut into bars 1 inch wide and 2 inches long.

Dutch Poppy Seed Bars

2½ sticks (1¼ cups) butter
1 cup sugar
¼ teaspoon almond extract
1½ cups ground almonds
3 cups sifted flour
½ teaspoon ginger
¼ teaspoon mace
1 egg, beaten
¾ cup poppy seeds

Grease an 11-by-16-inch jelly roll pan.

Cream the butter and sugar until light and fluffy. Blend in the almond extract and almonds, then the flour mixed with the ginger and mace. Pat into the pan. Chill 2 hours. Brush top with the egg and sprinkle with the poppy seeds, pressing them down lightly with the hand. Bake in a preheated 375° oven (with oven rack on middle level) 20 minutes or until delicately browned. Cool 5 minutes, then with a sharp knife cut into bars 1 inch wide and 2 inches long.

Coconut Shortbread

1½ cups sifted flour
¼ cup cornstarch
¾ cup sifted confectioners' sugar
½ pound (2 sticks) softened butter
1 teaspoon vanilla extract
2 cups fine grated coconut

Sift together the flour, cornstarch and confectioners' sugar. Blend in the butter and vanilla with the hand until a dough is formed. Chill 1 hour.

Break off small pieces of the dough and shape into walnut-sized balls. Roll in the coconut. Arrange on ungreased baking sheets, leaving 1 inch between each. Bake in a preheated 300° oven 20 minutes or until delicately browned. Remove from pan with a spatula.

Makes about 4 dozen cookies.

Scotch Shortbread

- *¾ cup (1½ sticks) sweet butter*
- *⅔ cup confectioners' sugar*
- *1¾ cups sifted flour*
- *½ teaspoon salt*

Preheat the oven to 325°.

Cream the butter; beat in the sugar gradually until very light and fluffy. Sift flour and salt over it and work in with the hand until thoroughly blended. Pat into the bottom of an 11-inch pie plate. Using a fluted pastry cutter or sharp knife, cut about halfway through the dough, making 24 wedges, then prick the tops with the tines of a fork. Bake on the middle rack 45 minutes or until pale yellow and firm to the touch in the center. Cool on a cake rack, then turn out, top side up, onto a board. Cut through the wedges where marked.

Puddings

Viennese Almond Pudding

(MANDELPUDDING)

¾ cup (1½ sticks) butter
¾ cup sugar
6 egg yolks
¾ cup ground blanched almonds
4 egg whites

Preheat oven to 350°.

Cream the butter, gradually beating in the sugar until light and fluffy. Add 1 egg yolk at a time, beating well after each addition. Beat in the almonds until mixture is very thick.

Beat the egg whites until stiff and fold into the nut mixture. Turn into a 1½-quart buttered baking dish. Bake 30 minutes or until puffed and browned. Serve at once, with whipped cream or Sabayon Sauce if desired.

Serves 6–8.

Steamed Almond Pudding

½ pound (2 sticks) butter
¾ cup sugar
6 egg yolks
1¼ cups finely ground blanched almonds
2 teaspoons grated lemon rind
6 egg whites, beaten stiff

Cream the butter until fluffy; gradually beat in the sugar, then the egg yolks, one at a time. Mix in the almonds and lemon rind. Fold in the egg whites. Turn into a buttered 2-quart mold. Tie a piece of aluminum foil over the mold, or if it has a lid, use it.

Place mold on a rack in a deep saucepan. Add enough boiling water to reach halfway up the mold. Cover the mold and cook 1 hour. Add boiling water to the saucepan from time to time to maintain the level. Carefully unmold and serve with Foamy Sauce or Ice Cream Sauce.

Serves 6–8.

Almond Pudding, Spanish Style

(PUDÍN DE ALMENDRAS)

½ cup currants
½ cup dry sherry
3 eggs
1 cup sugar
2 cups light cream
2 cups finely ground blanched almonds
1 teaspoon vanilla extract
¼ teaspoon mace

Preheat oven to 350°.

Soak the currants in the sherry 20 minutes; drain well. Beat the eggs in a bowl; gradually add the sugar, beating until light and fluffy. Mix in the cream, then the almonds, vanilla and mace. Turn into buttered custard cups. Place cups in a shallow pan of warm water. Bake 25 minutes or until set and lightly browned on top. Serve warm or cold, with Foamy Sauce if desired.

Serves 6.

French Cherry Pudding

(CLAFOUTIS LIMOUSIN)

2½ cups light cream
⅔ cup sifted flour
⅔ cup sifted confectioners' sugar
½ teaspoon salt
4 eggs, beaten
1 pound black cherries, pitted or 2½ cups canned, drained

Preheat oven to 400°.

Scald the cream and let cool. Sift the flour, sugar, and salt into a bowl. Make a well in the center and pour the eggs and cooled cream into it. Work in the flour mixture gradually, beating with a wooden spoon until very smooth. Mix in the cherries.

Turn into a well-buttered 2-quart baking dish. Bake 35 minutes, or until delicately browned and set. Sprinkle with confectioners' sugar and serve warm or cold. The pudding will fall, but the taste won't be affected.

Serves 6–8.

Scandinavian Cherry Pudding

1 cup sifted flour
1/8 teaspoon salt
1 teaspoon baking powder
1 16-ounce can pitted sour red cherries
3 tablespoons butter
1 1/4 cups sugar
3/4 cup milk
1/2 teaspoon almond extract

Preheat oven to 350°.

Sift together the flour, salt and baking powder. Drain the cherries, reserving 1/2 cup juice.

Cream the butter, gradually beating in 1 cup of the sugar until light and fluffy. Add the flour mixture, alternately with the milk, mixing until smooth. Pour into a buttered 8- by 8-inch baking dish.

Combine the cherries, reserved juice and remaining sugar. Bring to a boil, stirring until sugar dissolves. Mix in the almond extract and pour over the batter. Bake 30 minutes. Serve warm or cold with whipped cream.

Serves 6–8.

Swedish Lemon Pudding

4 egg yolks
1 cup sugar
1/3 cup lemon juice
4 egg whites
2 cups graham cracker crumbs

Beat the egg yolks in the top of a double boiler until light. Add half the sugar and beat until thick. Mix in the lemon juice. Place over hot water and cook, stirring constantly, until thick and smooth. Remove from the hot water.

Beat the egg whites until peaks form, then gradually beat in the remaining sugar until stiff. Fold into the hot lemon mixture. In a serving dish, make as many layers as possible of the lemon mixture and crumbs. Top layer should be crumbs. Chill until firm.

Serves 4–6.

Indian Lemon Pudding

¼ pound (1 stick) butter
1 cup sugar
6 egg yolks
4 tablespoons finely ground blanched almonds
⅓ cup lemon juice
6 egg whites

Preheat oven to 350°.

Cream the butter until fluffy. Gradually beat in the sugar. Add the egg yolks, beating until smooth. Mix in the almonds and lemon juice.

Beat the egg whites until stiff but not dry; fold into the lemon mixture. Turn into a buttered 2-quart baking dish. Bake 40 minutes or until puffed, brown and firm. Serve hot or cold. The pudding will fall a little.

Serves 4–6.

Swiss Apple Pudding

2 pounds tart apples, peeled and sliced
¼ cup dry white wine
½ cup sugar
½ teaspoon cinnamon
1 teaspoon grated lemond rind
4 cups fresh bread crumbs
⅔ cup firmly packed brown sugar
¼ pound (1 stick) butter

Preheat oven to 350°.

Cook the apples, wine, sugar, cinnamon, and lemon rind over low heat 15 minutes or until tender.

Mix the bread crumbs with the brown sugar, then cut in the butter (reserve 1 tablespoon). In a buttered baking dish, arrange alternate layers of the apples and bread crumb mixture, starting with the apples and ending with the crumbs. Dot with the reserved butter. Bake 30 minutes or until browned. Serve warm.

Serves 4–6.

Swedish Apple Pudding

4 cups peeled sliced apples
¼ teaspoon nutmeg
½ teaspoon cinnamon
1 cup sugar
1 cup sifted flour
¼ teaspoon salt
2 teaspoons baking powder
3 tablespoons butter
1 egg
½ cup milk
1 teaspoon vanilla extract

Preheat oven to 350°.

Toss the apples with a mixture of the nutmeg, cinnamon and half the sugar. Spread on the bottom of a buttered 2-quart baking dish.

Sift together the flour, salt and baking powder. Cream the butter, gradually beating in the remaining sugar. Beat in the egg. Add the flour mixture alternately with the milk, stirring until smooth. Add the vanilla. Pour over the apples. Bake 45 minutes or until batter is firm and browned. Serve warm with heavy cream.

Serves 6–8.

Middle Eastern Berry Rice Pudding

1 package frozen raspberries or strawberries
½ cup raw rice
¼ teaspoon salt
⅔ cup sugar
2 cups milk
2 cups light cream
4 eggs
2 cups heavy cream, whipped
2 tablespoons fruit liqueur

Thaw the berries and force through a sieve. You should have about 1 cup thick juice.

Combine the rice, salt, sugar, milk and cream in the top of a double boiler. Place over hot water and cook 45 minutes, or until very soft. Stir frequently.

Beat the eggs in a bowl; gradually add the rice mixture, stirring steadily to prevent curdling. Return to the double boiler and cook, stirring steadily until mixture coats the spoon. Turn into a bowl and cool. Mix in the berry juice, then fold in the whipped cream and liqueur. Chill 4 to 5 hours before serving.

Serves 6–8.

English Plum Pudding

3 cups fresh fine bread crumbs
⅔ cup firmly packed light brown sugar
¾ teaspoon salt
¾ teaspoon cinnamon
½ teaspoon nutmeg
¼ teaspoon ground cloves
¾ cup milk, scalded
6 eggs, beaten
⅓ cup beef fat (suet), ground
1 cup seedless raisins
¾ cup currants
¼ cup chopped dates
¼ cup chopped candied citron
¼ cup chopped candied orange peel
¼ cup chopped candied lemon peel
½ cup chopped apples
¼ cup cognac

To make the bread crumbs, trim sliced white bread. Tear the bread into small pieces and run in an electric blender, or force the bread through a foodmill.

Mix the bread crumbs, brown sugar, salt, cinnamon, nutmeg, and cloves. Add the scalded milk and let stand 15 minutes. Mix in the eggs and suet. Using your hands, mix in the fruits and cognac. Be sure the fruits are well distributed.

Turn into a greased 2-quart mold. Cover tightly with the lid or aluminum foil. Pour hot water to a depth of 1 inch into a pot with a cover. Place a rack in the pot and put the mold in it. Cover the pot and cook over low heat 6 hours, adding boiling water from time to time to maintain the water level. The plum pudding may be served at once, or it may be kept for a month or 2. Reheat in the same manner before serving. Serve with Hard Sauce.

Serves 10–12.

Cranberry Pudding

1½ cups fresh cranberries
1½ cups sifted flour
½ teaspoon salt
1 tablespoon baking powder
4 tablespoons (½ stick) butter
¾ cup sugar
1 egg, beaten
⅔ cup milk
1 teaspoon vanilla extract

Wash and dry the cranberries. Chop coarsely or put through the coarse blade of a food chopper. (If fresh cranberries are not available, use 2 cups whole canned cranberries, very well drained. Reduce sugar to ½ cup.)

Sift together the flour, salt and baking powder. Cream the butter; beat in the sugar until light and fluffy, then beat in the egg. Stir in the cranberries. Mix the milk and vanilla. Add to the cranberry mixture alternately with the flour mixture, mixing until blended after each addition.

Turn into a 1-quart mold and tie a piece of aluminum foil over it securely. Place on a rack in a deep saucepan. Add enough boiling water to reach halfway up the mold. Cover the saucepan and cook over low heat 1½ hours. Serve hot with whipped cream or Foamy Sauce.

Serves 6–8.

Coffee Rice Pudding with Meringue

¾ cup raw rice
3 cups water
4 egg yolks
½ teaspoon salt
1 cup sugar
5 teaspoons instant coffee
4 cups milk, scalded
4 egg whites
½ teaspoon vanilla extract

Preheat oven to 325°.

Bring the rice and water to a boil in a saucepan; cook over low heat 20 minutes or until tender.

Beat the eggs in the top of a double boiler; add the salt, and then gradually add ¾ cup of the sugar, beating until blended. Dissolve the coffee in the milk, then very gradually mix into the yolk mixture, stirring steadily to prevent curdling. Place over hot water and cook, stirring constantly until mixture coats the spoon. Remove from heat and mix with the rice. Turn into a buttered 1½-quart baking dish.

Beat the egg whites until soft peaks form, then gradually beat in the remaining sugar until meringue is stiff. Add the vanilla. Pile on top of the rice custard. Bake 15 minutes or until meringue is delicately browned.

Serves 6–8.

VARIATION

Vanilla Meringue Pudding: Omit the coffee and add 1 teaspoon vanilla extract.

Persian Rice Pudding

½ cup raw rice
2 cups milk
2 cups light cream
¾ cup sugar
¼ teaspoon salt
¼ teaspoon ground cardamom
2 eggs
½ cup chopped candied fruit
2 cups heavy cream

Combine the rice, milk, cream, sugar, salt and cardamom in the top of a double boiler. Place over hot water, cover and cook 1 hour, stirring frequently.

Beat the eggs in a bowl; gradually add the rice mixture, stirring steadily to prevent curdling. Return to double boiler and cook, stirring continuously until mixture coats the spoon. Remove from heat and stir in the fruit. Cool.

Whip the cream and fold into the rice mixture. Turn into a serving dish and chill.

Serves 8–10.

Austrian Baked Cottage Cheese Pudding

2 cups cottage cheese
2 hard-cooked egg yolks
3 raw egg yolks
1 cup sugar
3 tablespoons flour
4 tablespoons melted butter
1 teaspoon vanilla
⅓ cup currants
3 egg whites

Preheat oven to 325°.

Press all the liquid from the cheese. Force the cheese and hard-cooked egg yolks through a sieve.

Beat the egg yolks in a bowl. Gradually add the sugar, beating until light. Add the cheese mixture, flour, butter, vanilla and currants, mixing until well blended.

Beat the egg whites until stiff but not dry. Fold into the cheese mixture lightly.

Pour into a 2-quart baking dish. Bake 35 minutes or until firm and delicately browned. Serve warm or cold.

Serves 6–8.

Italian Cheese-Almond Pudding

(BUDINO DI FORMAGGIO)

1 pound cream cheese, softened
5 egg yolks
⅞ cup sugar
⅔ cup ground blanched almonds
⅓ cup chopped candied orange peel
2 teaspoons grated lemond rind

Preheat oven to 325°.

Beat the cheese in an electric mixer or blender until smooth, or force through a sieve. Beat the egg yolks and sugar until light, then beat in the cheese, almonds, orange peel and lemon rind. Turn into a buttered 7-inch spring form pan. Bake 45 minutes. Cool thoroughly before removing from spring form pan.

Serves 6–8.

Liqueur Pudding

4 eggs
½ cup sugar
½ cup sifted flour
3 cups milk
⅓ cup heavy cream
¼ cup plum, cherry or orange liqueur

Preheat oven to 400°.

Beat the eggs and sugar until light. Mix in the flour, then the milk, cream and liqueur. Turn into a buttered 1½-quart baking dish. Bake 30 minutes or until a knife inserted in the center comes out clean. Serve hot.

Serves 4–6.

Chilled Nougat Pudding, Italian Style

(TORRONE GELATO)

6 hard-cooked egg yolks
4 tablespoons butter, softened
⅓ cup sugar
2 tablespoons cognac
3 tablespoons cherry liqueur
24 ladyfingers, split
¾ cup sweet sherry
2 tablespoons unsweetened cocoa

Mash the egg yolks in an electric mixer or with a wooden spoon. Add the butter, beating until very fluffy and light. Gradually beat in the sugar until very light. Beat in the cognac very gradually, then the cherry liqueur. Beat until very smooth and light.

Soak the ladyfingers in the sherry. Line the bottom of a buttered oblong mold or pan with half the ladyfingers. Spread with half the yolk mixture. Beat the cocoa into the remaining half of the yolk mixture and spread over the plain mixture. Cover with remaining ladyfingers. Chill until very firm. Turn out onto a serving dish. Decorate with whipped cream if desired.

Serves 6–8.

Hungarian Puff Pudding

(UNGARISCHER PUDDING)

¼ pound (1 stick) butter
1 cup milk
½ teaspoon salt
3 tablespoons sugar
¾ cup sifted flour
4 egg yolks
2 teaspoons grated lemon rind
4 egg whites, beaten stiff

Preheat oven to 350°.

Butter a 1½-quart mold with 1 tablespoon of the butter, then dust it with flour.

Combine the milk, salt, sugar and remaining butter in a saucepan. Cook over low heat until butter melts, then add the flour all at once, beating with a wooden spoon, until mixture forms a ball and leaves the sides of the pan. Cool 5 minutes, then add 1 egg yolk at a time, beating after each addition until smooth. Stir in the lemon rind, then fold in the egg whites.

Turn into the prepared mold. Place mold in a shallow pan of hot water. Bake 1 hour or until browned and set. Immediately run a spatula around the edge and unmold onto a heated serving dish. Serve with Berry Sauce or French Sauce.

Serves 6–8.

Trinidad Pudding

4 egg whites
¼ teaspoon salt
1 teaspoon cream of tartar
1 cup sugar
¾ teaspoon powdered ginger
1 cup fine graham cracker crumbs
½ cup finely grated coconut
½ cup finely chopped pecans or walnuts

Preheat oven to 350°.

Beat the egg whites, salt and cream of tartar until soft peaks form. Very gradually beat in the sugar until mixture is stiff. Fold in a mixture of the ginger, graham cracker crumbs, coconut and nuts. Turn into a buttered deep 9-inch pie plate. Bake 30 minutes or until puffed, browned and set. Serve warm with whipped cream.

Serves 6–8.

Hasty Pudding

4 cups milk
1 teaspoon salt
½ cup yellow cornmeal
3 tablespoons butter
½ cup molasses
½ teaspoon nutmeg

Preheat oven to 350°.

Bring 2 cups of the milk and the salt to a boil in a saucepan; gradually stir in the cornmeal. Cook, stirring constantly, until thickened. Remove from the heat and mix in the butter, molasses, nutmeg and remaining milk. Turn into a buttered 2-quart baking dish. Cover the dish and bake 3 hours. Serve with whipped or plain cream or vanilla ice cream.

Serves 6.

Note: One-half cup peeled diced apples or ¼ cup seedless raisins may be added to the unbaked mixture, if you like.

English Treacle Pudding

1½ cups sifted flour
½ teaspoon powdered ginger
¼ teaspoon nutmeg
¼ teaspoon salt
1 teaspoon baking soda
1 egg
2 tablespoons sugar
½ cup molasses
2 tablespoons melted butter
½ cup boiling water

Sift together the flour, ginger, nutmeg, salt and baking soda.

Beat the egg until thick, then beat in the sugar and molasses. Mix in the butter. Add the flour mixture alternately with the boiling water, stirring until smooth. Turn into a greased 1½-quart mold or a coffee can. Tie a piece of aluminum foil over the top.

Place the mold on a trivet or rack in a deep saucepan. Add boiling water to reach halfway up the mold. Cover the pan and cook over medium heat 1½ hours. Unmold and serve with Hard Sauce or Sabayon Sauce.

Serves 6–8.

Burmese Sago (Tapioca) Sweet

4 cups water
1 cup sugar
1 cup quick-cooking tapioca
2 teaspoons green food coloring
2 cups finely grated coconut

Bring the water and sugar to a boil; stir in the tapioca and cook until transparent. Add the coloring. Pour into a greased 8-by-8-inch pan. Chill. Cut into small squares and dip in the coconut.

Serves 8–10.

Raisin Pudding, Brittany Style

(FAR À LA BRETONNE)

2 cups sifted flour
1/8 teaspoon salt
6 eggs
1 1/4 cups sugar
3 cups milk
1 cup light cream
2 tablespoons cognac
1 cup seedless raisins

Preheat oven to 450°.

Sift the flour and salt into a bowl. Work in 1 egg at a time. Beat in the sugar, then gradually stir in the milk, cream and cognac. The batter will be very thin.

Spread the raisins on the bottom of a buttered 11-by-18-inch baking pan. Pour the batter over them slowly. Bake in a preheated 450° oven for 15 minutes, then reduce heat to 257° and bake 1 hour longer or until set and browned. Cool 20 minutes, then chill and cut into squares.

Serves 8–10.

Javanese Coconut Cups

¾ cup flaked coconut
1½ cups heavy cream
3 tablespoons butter
¾ cup sugar
¼ cup sifted flour
½ teaspoon powdered ginger
6 egg yolks
6 egg whites

Preheat oven to 350°.

Combine the coconut and cream in a saucepan. Bring to a boil, remove from heat and let stand 30 minutes. Strain the cream, pressing through firmly. Discard the coconut.

Cream the butter; beat in the sugar until light. Sift in the flour and ginger, mixing until smooth. Add 1 egg yolk at a time, beating well after each addition. Gradually stir in the coconut cream.

Beat the egg whites until stiff but not dry. Fold into the yolk mixture. Spoon into 8 to 10 buttered custard cups. Place the cups in a shallow pan of hot water. Bake 45 minutes or until set. Cool, then chill. Remove from the cups.

Serves 8–10.

Hawaiian Sweet Potato Pudding

2 cups light cream
1½ cups flaked coconut
1 29-ounce can sweet potatoes, drained
½ teaspoon salt
¼ cup sugar
2 tablespoons butter

Combine the cream and 1 cup of the coconut in a saucepan; bring to a boil, remove from heat and let soak 30 minutes. Drain, pressing all the cream from the coconut. Discard coconut.

Mash the sweet potatoes until smooth. Beat in the salt, sugar and coconut cream. Spread in a buttered 9-inch pie plate. Bake in a preheated 400° oven 20 minutes or until lightly browned.

While the pudding is baking, sauté the remaining coconut in the butter until lightly browned, stirring constantly. Sprinkle on top of the baked pudding. Serve warm or cold.

Serves 6–8.

Virgin Island Sweet Potato Custard Pudding

1 pound sweet potatoes
¾ cup (1½ sticks) butter
½ teaspoon salt
1 cup firmly packed brown sugar
2 eggs
2 tablespoons grated orange rind
½ teaspoon powdered ginger
½ teaspoon nutmeg
2 tablespoons dark rum

Preheat oven to 350°.

Peel and grate the sweet potatoes. You should have 2 cups.

Cream the butter and salt, gradually adding the sugar; beat until light and fluffy. Beat in 1 egg at a time, then mix in the sweet potatoes, orange rind, ginger, nutmeg and rum. Turn into a buttered 8-by-12-inch baking dish. Bake 1 hour. Serve warm, cut into squares, topped with rum-flavored whipped cream.

Serves 4–6.

Polynesian Sweet Potato-Pineapple Pudding

4 cups mashed cooked sweet potatoes
3 tablespoons butter
½ cup honey
½ cup heavy cream
½ teaspoon salt
½ teaspoon powdered ginger
3 egg yolks, beaten
1 cup drained, canned crushed pineapple
3 egg whites, beaten stiff

Preheat oven to 325°.

Beat together the potatoes, butter, honey, cream, salt and ginger. Beat in the egg yolks, then stir in the pineapple. Fold in the egg whites. Turn into a buttered 2-quart baking dish. Bake 1 hour or until browned and set. Serve warm, with whipped cream if desired.

Serves 6–8.

Mousses

Raspberry Mousse

(MOUSSE AUX FRAMBOISES)

1 envelope (1 tablespoon) gelatin
⅓ cup orange juice
2 packages frozen raspberries, thawed
¼ cup sugar
2 tablespoons fruit liqueur
2 egg whites
1½ cups heavy cream, whipped

Soften the gelatin in the orange juice. Drain the raspberries well. Measure the juice and add water, if necessary, to make 1 cup liquid. Cook the juice and sugar in a saucepan over low heat until syrupy. Add the raspberries and cook 10 minutes. Add the gelatin and mix until dissolved. Force through a sieve. Cool. Stir in the liqueur.

Beat the egg whites until stiff but not dry and fold into the raspberry purée. Fold in the whipped cream. Pour into a 1½-quart mold and chill until firm.

Serves 6–8.

Frozen Fruit Mousse

(BOMBE AUX FRUITS)

¾ cup chopped candied fruits
¼ cup cognac
¾ cup sugar
½ cup water
4 egg yolks
½ cup chopped almonds
2 cups heavy cream

Marinate the fruits in the cognac 30 minutes.

Bring the sugar and water to a boil; cook 5 minutes, or until thick and syrupy. Cool. Beat the egg yolks in the top of a double boiler, gradually stir in the syrup; place over hot water and cook, stirring steadily until mixture is thick and coats spoon. Strain through a fine sieve. Cool. Mix in the undrained fruits and the nuts.

Whip the cream and fold it into the mixture. Turn into a 1½-quart *bombe* or other mold. Cover with a piece of buttered waxed paper, then with the mold cover. Freeze until set, about 6 hours. Unmold onto a chilled serving dish. Decorate with whipped cream and candied fruits if desired.

Serves 6–8.

Chocolate Mousse

(MOUSSE AU CHOCOLAT)

¼ pound sweet chocolate
3 tablespoons brewed coffee
4 egg yolks
¼ cup sugar
1 teaspoon vanilla extract
4 egg whites, beaten stiff
1½ cups heavy cream, whipped

Break the chocolate into small pieces and combine with the coffee in the top of a double boiler. Place over hot water until melted and smooth. Cool.

Beat the egg yolks in a bowl; add the sugar, beating until light and fluffy. Stir in the chocolate mixture and vanilla. Fold in the egg whites gently but thoroughly and then the whipped cream. Turn into a 1½-quart mold. Chill until set.

Serves 6–8.

Mocha Mousse

½ pound (8 squares) semi-sweet chocolate
½ cup double-strength brewed coffee
3 tablespoons crème de cacao (cordial)
2 cups heavy cream
½ cup sugar

Break the chocolate into small pieces and combine in a sauce-pan with the brewed coffee. Place over low heat and let melt, stirring frequently. Cool. Stir in the crème de cacao.

Whip the cream until it begins to thicken, then add the sugar and continue whipping until it holds its shape. Fold in the choco-late mixture; turn into a 1½-quart mold. Cover with aluminum foil. Chill until set.

Serves 6–8.

Frozen Sabayon

(MOUSSE GLACÉE SABAYON)

8 egg yolks
1 cup superfine sugar
½ cup Marsala or sweet sherry
2 cups heavy cream, whipped

Beat the egg yolks in the top of a double boiler. Add the sugar and wine; place over hot water and beat with a wire whisk or fork until thickened. Remove from heat and beat until cold. Fold in the whipped cream. Turn into a mold and freeze until firm.

Serves 8–10.

Chocolate-Orange Mousse

(MOUSSELINE AU CHOCOLAT)

6 ounces (6 squares) semi-sweet chocolate
¼ cup orange juice
6 ounces (1½ sticks) sweet butter, at room temperature
4 egg yolks
¾ cup superfine sugar
¼ cup Grand Marnier or Curaçao
¼ cup finely diced candied orange peel
1½ cups heavy cream, whipped

Melt the chocolate in the orange juice in the top of a double boiler over hot water. Add 2 tablespoons of butter at a time, beating after each addition.

In a bowl, beat the egg yolks and sugar until very thick. Beat in the liqueur, then place over hot water and beat until mixture is hot. Remove from the heat and continue beating until cool. Beat in the chocolate mixture, then stir in the orange peel. Fold in the whipped cream. Turn into a 1½-quart mold and chill until firm.

Serves 8–10.

Champagne Mousse

2 envelopes (2 tablespoons) gelatin
¼ cup water
8 eggs
1 cup sugar
2 cups champagne or dry white wine
1½ cups heavy cream, whipped

Soften the gelatin in the water. Separate 5 of the eggs. Beat 5 egg yolks and the remaining 3 whole eggs together in the top of a double boiler. Beat in the sugar, and then the champagne. Place over hot water and cook, stirring steadily, until thickened. Mix in the gelatin until dissolved. Cool.

Beat the reserved egg whites until stiff but not dry. Fold into the champagne mixture with the whipped cream. Turn into a 2½-quart mold or soufflé dish. Chill until firm.

Serves 8–10.

Austrian Frozen Sour Cream Mousse

2 ounces sweet chocolate
2 cups sour cream
½ cup sugar
¼ cup macaroon crumbs
1 tablespoon rum
1 teaspoon vanilla extract

Break the chocolate into small pieces, and melt in the top of a double boiler over hot water, stirring until smooth. Cool.

Mix the sour cream with the sugar, then blend in the chocolate, macaroon crumbs, rum and vanilla. Turn into a small mold and freeze until firm.

Serves 4–6.

Austrian Cream Cheese Mousse

(TOPFENCREME)

1 pound cream cheese, softened
½ cup confectioners' sugar
4 egg yolks
1 cup heavy cream
1 teaspoon vanilla extract
4 egg whites, beaten stiff

Beat the cheese until smooth, then beat in the confectioners' sugar. Add 1 egg yolk at a time, beating after each addition. Beat in the cream and vanilla until mixture is very stiff. Fold in the egg whites.

Rinse a 1½-quart mold with cold water, shake out but don't dry, and pour the mixture into it. Freeze until firm, then unmold. Surround with strawberries or raspberries.

Serves 8–10.

Rice Mousse Ring

MOUSSE

¾ cup raw rice
3 cups milk
1 cup light cream
¾ cup sugar
½ teaspoon salt
2 envelopes (2 tablespoons) gelatin
¼ cup fruit liqueur
1 cup heavy cream, whipped

Bring the rice, milk, cream, sugar and salt to a boil; cook over low heat 25 minutes, stirring frequently. Purée in an electric blender or force through a sieve. Soften the gelatin in the liqueur, then stir into the hot rice mixture until dissolved. Cool, then fold in the whipped cream. Turn into a 9-inch ring mold. Chill until set. Unmold onto a chilled serving dish. Fill the center with the berries.

BERRIES

2 cups raspberries or strawberries
⅓ cup sugar
2 tablespoons fruit liqueur

Mix the berries, sugar and liqueur (same flavor as used in mousse). Chill 1 hour.

Serves 6–8.

Pastries

Flaky Pastry

2 cups sifted flour
¾ teaspoon salt
¾ cup shortening
6 tablespoons ice water

Sift the flour and salt into a bowl. Using a pastry blender or two knives, cut in ½ cup of the shortening until the consistency of coarse corn meal. Break up the remaining shortening and cut in until mixture is the size of peas. Sprinkle with a little water and toss with a fork, adding just enough water to make the flour mixture cling together. Wrap in a damp cloth and chill 30 minutes.

Divide dough in two, making one piece slightly larger than the other. On a lightly floured surface, roll out the larger piece as thin as possible. Fit into an ungreased 9-inch pie plate. Trim the edges. Brush edges with water or egg white. Fill with selected filling. Roll out the remaining pastry as thin as possible. Cut a few slits in the top. Cover the filling with the pastry. Press edges together on the rim to seal; fold edge of top crust under bottom and flute or press with the tines of a fork. Bake as directed for each recipe.

VARIATION

Cheese Pastry: Add ½ cup Cheddar Cheese with the remaining shortening. Proceed as directed.

French Tart Paste

(PÂTE SUCRÉE)

1 cup sifted flour
1/8 teaspoon salt
1 tablespoon sugar
1/4 pound (1 stick) sweet butter, at room temperature
1 egg yolk
1 tablespoon ice water

Sift the flour, salt and sugar into a bowl; make a well in the center. Place the butter, egg yolk and water in the well; work in the flour with the hand until a ball of dough is formed. Chill 2 hours or overnight. Roll out 1/8 inch thick on a lightly floured surface and fit into a buttered 9-inch pie plate or *flan* ring. (This is a metal ring with straight sides and no bottom. The ring is placed on a buttered baking sheet.) Flute the edges and chill 30 minutes before filling. To prebake the shell, prick the bottom in several places with a fork and place a pie plate or waxed paper covered with rice or beans over it to keep from shrinking. Bake in a preheated 400° oven 20 minutes or until browned. Remove the weight and cool.

Sour Cream Pastry

2 cups sifted flour
1/4 teaspoon salt
1/2 pound (2 sticks) butter or margarine
6 tablespoons sour cream

Sift the flour and salt into a bowl. With a pastry blender or two knives, cut in the butter until mixture forms pieces the size of peas. Blend in the sour cream until a ball of dough is formed. Wrap in foil or waxed paper; chill overnight or at least 2 hours. Roll out and proceed as directed for each recipe.

Makes enough for a 2-crust 9-inch pie.

Walnut Pastry

1¼ cups sifted flour
⅛ teaspoon salt
¾ cup finely ground walnuts
¼ pound (1 stick) butter or margarine
4 tablespoons ice water

Sift the flour and salt into bowl; mix in the walnuts. Using a pastry blender or 2 knives, cut in the butter until mixture is like coarse corn meal. Gradually add the water, tossing lightly until particles stick together. (It may not be necessary to add all the water.) Form into a ball and chill 2 hours before rolling. Proceed as directed in each recipe.

Makes enough for a 2-crust 9-inch pie.

Meringue Pastry Shell, Paris Style

3 egg whites
⅛ teaspoon salt
¼ teaspoon cream of tartar
¾ cup very fine granulated sugar
1 teaspoon vanilla extract

Preheat oven to 300°.

Have the egg whites at room temperature. Beat the egg whites and salt until foamy. Add the cream of tartar and beat until soft peaks are formed. Add 2 tablespoons of sugar at a time, beating until very stiff. Beat in the vanilla. Spread the meringue over the bottom and sides of a 9-inch pie plate, piling it about 1 inch above the edge of the plate. Bake 45 minutes or until delicately browned and dry. Carefully loosen the shell from the pan while warm, but leave in pie plate. Cool thoroughly before filling. Use with any filling which does not require baking.

VARIATION

Coconut Meringue Shell: Toss ⅔ cup fine-grated coconut with 3 tablespoons sifted confectioners' sugar to coat coconut. Fold into the meringue and proceed as directed.

Graham Cracker Pastry Shell

1¼ cups fine graham cracker crumbs
2 tablespoons sugar
⅓ cup melted cooled butter or margarine

Preheat oven to 375°.

Mix all the ingredients together. Press firmly on the bottom and sides of a 9-inch pie plate. Bake 6 minutes; cool before filling. For unbaked shell, chill 1 hour before filling.

VARIATIONS

Gingersnap Crumb Pastry Shell

1¼ cups fine gingersnap crumbs
3 tablespoons sugar
¼ cup melted cooled butter or margarine

Proceed as directed for Graham Cracker Pastry Shell.

Chocolate Crumb Pastry Shell

1¼ cups chocolate cooky crumbs
2 tablespoons sugar
¼ cup melted cooled butter or margarine

Proceed as directed for Graham Cracker Pastry Shell.

Zwieback Pastry Shell

1¼ cups fine zwieback crumbs
2 tablespoons sugar
⅓ cup melted cooled butter or margarine

Proceed as directed for Graham Cracker Pastry Shell.

Hungarian Strudel

DOUGH

2½ cups flour
½ teaspoon salt
2 teaspoons vinegar
½ cup vegetable oil
2 egg whites
½ cup warm water

Sift the flour and salt together into a bowl. Make a well in the center. Into it put the vinegar, ¼ cup oil and egg whites. Gradually work in the flour, adding just enough of the warm water to make a soft dough. It may not be necessary to add all the water. Knead well; raise the dough and slap it down several times until it loses its stickiness. This will take 10–15 minutes. Form into a ball, brush with oil and cover with a warm bowl for 30 minutes.

Spread a cloth over a large table and dust with flour. Roll out the dough in a circle, turning it several times. Brush with oil. Flour both hands heavily and begin stretching the dough from underneath with the backs of the hands. Work carefully and brush with more oil occasionally. Don't worry if the dough tears; it should be almost transparent. Cut off the thick edges. Let dry for 5 minutes.

CHEESE FILLING

¼ pound (1 stick) butter
¾ cup sugar
6 egg yolks
1¾ cups sour cream
2 teaspoons grated lemon rind
1 pound cream cheese
½ cup seedless raisins (optional)
6 egg whites, beaten stiff

Melt half the butter and brush the dough with it.

Cream the remaining butter, gradually adding the sugar. Add the egg yolks, beating until light and fluffy. Add the sour cream and lemon rind. Force the cheese through a sieve. Combine with previous mixture, beating until thoroughly smooth. Add the raisins if desired. Fold in the egg whites. Spread the cheese mixture over two-thirds of the dough. Turn opposite sides in and roll up loosely. Brush with melted butter. Place on a buttered baking sheet. Bake in a preheated 375° oven 45 minutes or until delicately browned. Cut into 2-inch slices while hot.

APPLE FILLING

3 tablespoons butter
1½ cups fresh bread crumbs
¾ cup melted butter
¾ cup ground walnuts
4 cups peeled sliced apples
1 cup seedless raisins (optional)
2 teaspoons grated lemon rind
⅔ cup sugar
1 tablespoon cinnamon

Melt the 3 tablespoons butter in a skillet; sauté the bread crumbs in it until lightly browned. Cool.

Brush the strudel dough generously with melted butter. Sprinkle with the bread crumbs and walnuts. Spread the apples in a 2-inch strip along one end of the dough. Brush with melted butter and sprinkle with the raisins, lemon rind, sugar and cinnamon. Fold in opposite sides of the dough. Starting from the apple end, lift up the cloth, and roll up like a jelly roll. Transfer the roll to a greased baking sheet. (If roll is too long for the pan, turn ends in.) Brush with melted butter. Bake in a preheated

350° oven 50 minutes or until delicately browned. Brush with melted butter a few times during the baking period. Sprinkle top with sugar. Serve warm, cut into 2-inch pieces.

POPPY SEED FILLING

½ pound poppy seeds
¼ pound (1 stick) butter
½ cup honey
1½ cups coarsely chopped walnuts or pecans
½ cup seedless raisins
¼ cup heavy cream
1 tablespoon grated orange rind

Have the poppy seeds ground where you buy them, or cover with boiling water and let soak 2 hours, then drain well and grind twice, using the finest blade of the meat chopper.

Cream the butter; beat in the honey, nuts, raisins, cream and orange rind. Proceed as directed.

French Puff Paste

(PÂTE FEUILLETÉE)

4 cups sifted flour
1¼ cups ice water (about)
1 teaspoon salt
1 tablespoon lemon juice
1 pound (4 sticks) sweet butter

Sift the flour onto a board and make a well in the center. Pour 1 cup ice water, the salt and lemon juice into it and work in the flour, until a firm dough is formed. If too dry, add a little more water. Knead and pound dough until smooth and elastic. Cover with a bowl for 10 minutes. Roll out into a rectangle about 10 by 18 inches. Shape the butter into a square and place it in the center. Fold the dough over the butter, wrap in a napkin and chill 15 minutes. Roll into a long strip, being careful not to let the butter break through. Fold in thirds; open edges toward you. Roll and fold again. Chill for 30 minutes. Repeat the process three times, always keeping the open edges out and never exposing the butter. Chill for at least two hours before using as directed in recipes using puff paste.

Napoleons

(MILLEFEUILLES)

Puff Paste Recipe
Crème Pâtissière Recipe
Confectioners' sugar

Preheat oven to 375°.

Divide the pastry into thirds. Roll out ¼ inch thick and cut into 3-inch wide strips. Place on baking sheets and prick the surface of the pastry. Bake 40 minutes. Cool on a cake rack. Put the layers together with the pastry cream between, or you may use sweetened whipped cream and strawberries. Dust top with confectioners' sugar. Cut in 2-inch slices, using great care.

Serves 10–12.

Note: The dough may be cut into individual serving-sized pieces before baking, if you prefer. Bake 20 minutes or until browned.

Peach Turnover

2 pounds peaches
3 tablespoons butter
¼ cup sugar
1 tablespoon cognac
1 teaspoon vanilla
½ teaspoon almond extract
Puff Paste recipe
1 egg, beaten

Peel and slice the peaches. Melt the butter in a saucepan. Add the peaches and sugar and cook over low heat 5 minutes, stirring frequently. Add the cognac, vanilla and almond extract. Taste for sweetening—if too tart, add a little sugar. Cool. Preheat the oven to 425°.

Roll out the puff paste into a 12-inch circle ¼ inch thick. Place the peaches in the center. Fold over the dough, moisten the edges with water and press together. Place on a baking sheet; brush the top with the egg.

Bake 30 minutes or until browned. Serve warm.

Cream Puffs

(PÂTE À CHOUX)

¼ pound butter
1 cup water
1 teaspoon sugar
⅛ teaspoon salt
1⅛ cups sifted flour
3 eggs
1 egg yolk

Cook the butter, water, sugar and salt in a saucepan until butter melts and is boiling. Add the flour all at once, and cook over very low heat, stirring constantly until mixture forms a ball and leaves the sides of the pan. Remove from the heat and add the eggs and egg yolk, one at a time, beating with a wooden spoon after each addition until mixture is glossy.

For large cream puffs, drop by the tablespoon onto a buttered baking sheet, leaving 1 inch between each. Bake in a preheated 400° oven 10 minutes. Reduce the heat to 300° and bake 25 minutes longer or until browned and no beads of moisture remain. Cool before splitting and filling with ice cream, whipped cream or Crème Pâtissière.

Makes 12–14.

For small cream puffs (*profiteroles*), drop by the teaspoon onto a buttered baking sheet, leaving ½ inch between each. Bake in a preheated 400° oven 10 minutes; reduce the heat to 300° and bake 15 minutes longer or until browned and free from drops of moisture.

Makes about 36.

For Eclairs, force through a pastry tube with a flat end into strips 4 by 1 inches or shape with 2 spoons. Bake as directed for large cream puffs.

Pyramid Cake, French Style

(CROQUEMBOUCHE)

1½ cups water
¼ pound (1 stick) butter
1 cup sifted flour
¼ teaspoon salt
4 eggs
1 cup heavy cream
2 tablespoons confectioners' sugar
3 tablespoons orange liqueur
⅔ cup granulated sugar
⅛ teaspoon cream of tartar
1 cup hot water

Preheat the oven to 400°.

Bring one cup of the water and the butter to a boil in a saucepan. Add the flour and salt all at once. Cook over low heat, stirring with a wooden spoon until the mixture forms a ball and leaves the sides of the pan. Remove the pan from the heat. Add the eggs, one at a time, beating very well until the mixture is thick and shiny. Place the batter in rounded teaspoonfuls 1 inch apart on an ungreased cooky sheet. Bake 30 minutes or until crisp and lightly golden. Cook on a cake rack. Make a small hole in the base of each puff. Whip the cream until peaks form, sweeten with the confectioners' sugar and fold in the liqueur. Using a pastry bag and a plain tube, fill the puffs with the whipped cream by inserting the point of the tube into the hole in the base of each, or use a small spoon.

Place the sugar, remaining half cup of water and the cream of tartar in a small skillet. Bring to a boil, stirring constantly. Lower the heat and cook until a light amber color, stirring occasionally. Keep the syrup warm over very low heat while building the pyramid. Roll a cream puff in the warm syrup and set it, top (intact) side facing out, around the outer edge of a 9-inch, flat, round plate. Continue and form a ring around the edge of the plate. Fill in the center with more puffs. Over the spaces between the puffs in the first row, make a slightly smaller circle of dipped puffs. Fill in the center again. Continue until there is a total of five circles. Top with one cream puff.

Add one cup hot water to the syrup left in the skillet. Cook slowly, stirring occasionally, to 232° on a candy thermometer. Cool the syrup to room temperature and drizzle it down the sides of the pyramid. Serve the *croquembouche* immediately, from the top, or refrigerate until needed.

Serves 10–12.

South American Coconut Pastries

(PASTELITOS DE COCO)

2 cups flour
½ teaspoon salt
½ teaspoon baking powder
¼ pound (1 stick) butter
¼ cup orange juice
1½ cups flaked coconut
1 tablespoon cornstarch
½ cup sugar
¾ cup light cream
2 egg yolks
3 tablespoons melted butter, cooled
1 egg white

Sift the flour, salt and baking powder into a bowl; cut in the butter with a pastry blender or 2 knives until the consistency of coarse cornmeal. Mix in the orange juice until a ball of dough is formed. Chill 1 hour.

Mix together the coconut, cornstarch, sugar and cream. Cook over low heat, stirring constantly for 5 minutes. Beat the egg yolks and melted butter in a bowl; gradually add the hot mixture, stirring constantly. Return to saucepan and stir over low heat for 2 minutes. Cool.

Roll out the dough as thin as possible on a lightly floured surface. Cut into circles with a 3-inch cooky cutter. Place a tablespoon of the coconut mixture on half the circle and cover with the remaining circles. Seal the edges with a little water. Arrange on a baking sheet and brush with the egg white. Bake in a preheated 425° oven 10 minutes or until delicately browned. Cool on a cake rack.

Makes about 2 dozen.

Danish Pastry

DOUGH

1 package yeast
2 tablespoons sugar
¼ cup lukewarm water
2 cups flour
½ teaspoon salt
3 egg yolks, beaten
½ teaspoon vanilla extract
½ cup milk, scalded and cooled
½ pound (2 sticks) butter

Dissolve the yeast and sugar in the water. Sift flour and salt into a bowl. Make a well in the center and into it put the yeast mixture, egg yolks, vanilla, milk and 2 tablespoons butter, cut in small pieces. Mix with the fingers until a medium-soft dough is formed, then knead until smooth and elastic. Chill 15 minutes.

Shape the remaining butter into two oblongs, about ¼ inch thick. On a floured surface, roll out the dough into a rectangle about 8 by 20 inches. Place one piece of butter in the center. Fold one long end over the butter and place second piece of butter on top. Fold the other end of dough over it. Press open edges together. Roll out carefully from the short end into a rectangle. Flour the surface again to keep dough from sticking. Brush excess flour from dough and fold long ends over each other. Wrap the dough in waxed paper or foil and chill 30 minutes. Repeat rolling and chilling 3 more times, always rolling from the open ends. Chill 2 hours before final rolling and baking as directed in recipes.

CHEESE FILLING

¼ pound cream cheese
½ cup cottage cheese, drained
¼ cup sugar
1 egg yolk
2 tablespoons sour cream
½ teaspoon vanilla extract
2 tablespoons white raisins (optional)
3 tablespoons heavy cream

Beat all the ingredients together until smooth.

Roll out the Danish Pastry dough ⅛ inch thick. Cut into 4-inch squares. Put a teaspoon of the filling on each. Bring two opposite corners of the dough over the filling and press together firmly. Arrange on greased baking sheets. Chill 20 minutes. Brush with the cream or beaten egg yolk mixed with the cream.

Bake in a preheated 450° oven 10 minutes. Reduce heat to 350° and bake 10 minutes longer or until browned.

Makes about 18.

PRUNE FILLING

1 pound cooked prunes, pitted
½ cup coarsely chopped walnuts or pecans
3 tablespoons melted butter
2 tablespoons grated orange rind
3 tablespoons sugar

Chop the prunes and mix in all the remaining ingredients. Proceed as directed above.

NUT FILLING

2 eggs
⅓ cup sugar
⅓ cup melted butter
1½ cups ground almonds, walnuts, pecans or filberts
1 teaspoon vanilla extract

Beat the eggs and sugar until thick and light. Mix in the butter, nuts and vanilla. Proceed as directed above.

CINNAMON SLICES

½ cup currants
2 tablespoons cognac
1 egg, beaten
¾ cup sugar
2 teaspoons cinnamon
¾ cup coarsely chopped walnuts

Soak the currants in the cognac 10 minutes. Drain.

Roll out the dough ⅛ inch thick and into a rectangle 5 inches wide by 16 inches long. Brush with the egg, reserving a little. Sprinkle with a mixture of the sugar and cinnamon, then with the currants and nuts. Press the filling down lightly. Roll up like a jelly roll. Seal edges with reserved yolk. Cut into ¾-inch slices. Arrange on a lightly greased baking sheet; flatten slices slightly. Bake as directed.

Makes about 20.

Pies

Blueberry Pie

2 12-ounce packages frozen blueberries, thawed
¼ cup minute tapioca
⅓ cup sugar
¼ teaspoon salt
¼ teaspoon cinnamon
1 tablespoon lemon juice
Pastry for 2-crust 9-inch pies
1 tablespoon butter

Preheat oven to 425°.

Drain the berries well, reserving ½ cup juice. Combine the reserved juice, berries, tapioca, sugar, salt, cinnamon and lemon juice. Let stand 15 minutes. Roll out a little more than half the pastry as thin as possible; line a 9-inch pie plate with it. Fill the shell with the berry mixture. Dot with the butter. Roll out the remaining pastry, cut a few slits in the top and fit over the fruit, sealing the edges well. Bake 50 minutes or until browned. Cool on a cake rack.

Berry Pie

Pastry for 2-crust pie
4 cups blueberries, raspberries, strawberries or blackberries, washed and drained
1 tablespoon cornstarch
¾ cup sugar
⅛ teaspoon salt
2 teaspoons lemon juice

Preheat oven to 425°. Line a 9-inch pie plate with a little more than half the pastry.

Lightly toss together the berries, cornstarch, sugar, salt and lemon juice. Fill the lined pie plate. Roll out the remaining pastry and cut a few slits in the top. Cover the fruit, sealing the edges well. For a glossy crust, brush with cream or beaten egg yolk. Bake 45 minutes or until browned. Cool on a cake rack.

Fresh Red Cherry Pie

4 cups fresh pitted sour red cherries
2 tablespoons cornstarch
1¼ cups sugar
Pastry for 2-crust pie

Preheat oven to 400°.

Combine the cherries, cornstarch and sugar in a saucepan; cook over low heat, stirring constantly to the boiling point. Cook 5 minutes longer, stirring occasionally. Cool. Line a 9-inch pie plate with a little more than half the pastry. Fill with the cherries. Roll out remaining pastry, cut a few slits in the top and cover the fruit, sealing the edges well. Or cut the pastry into strips and form into a lattice covering. Bake 45 minutes or until browned. Cool on a cake rack.

Canned Red Cherry Pie

1 No. 2 can pitted sour cherries
2 tablespoons minute tapioca
¾ cup sugar
Dash salt
⅛ teaspoon almond extract
Pastry for 2-crust pie

Preheat oven to 400°.

Drain the cherries, reserving 1 cup juice. Combine the cherries, reserved juice, tapioca, sugar, salt and almond extract. Let stand 15 minutes. Line a 9-inch pie plate with a little more than half the pastry. Fill with the cherry mixture. Cover with remaining pastry, sealing the edges well. Cut a few slits in the top. Bake 45 minutes or until browned. Cool on a cake rack.

Apple Pie

Pastry for 2-crust pie
6 cups thinly sliced tart apples, peeled
¾ cup sugar
1 teaspoon cinnamon or nutmeg
2 tablespoons butter or margarine

Preheat oven to 425°. Line a 9-inch pie plate with a little more than half the pastry.

Toss together the apples, sugar and cinnamon. Fill the prepared pie plate. Dot with the butter. Roll out the remaining pastry, cut slits in it and cover the apples, sealing the edges well. For a glossy crust, brush with cream or beaten egg. Bake 45 minutes or until browned.

VARIATION

Apple-Cheese Pie: Prepare Cheese Pastry, and proceed as directed above, omitting the cinnamon or nutmeg.

Apple Custard Pie

4 teaspoons cornstarch
1/8 teaspoon salt
1 cup sugar
2 eggs, beaten
1/2 cup heavy cream, whipped
2 cups chopped apples
1 9-inch unbaked pastry shell
4 tablespoons butter
1/4 cup sifted flour
3/4 teaspoon cinnamon
1/8 teaspoon nutmeg

Preheat oven to 450°.

Sift together the cornstarch, salt and 3/4 cup sugar. Beat in the eggs until smooth, then stir in the whipped cream and apples. Spread in the pie shell. Bake 10 minutes, reduce heat to 350° and bake 20 minutes longer. While the pie is baking, mix together the butter, flour, cinnamon, nutmeg and remaining sugar until the consistency of crumbs. Spread over the pie and bake 10 minutes longer or until browned. Cool.

Coconut Custard Pie

4 eggs
1/4 teaspoon salt
1/3 cup sugar
2 cups milk
1 cup light cream
1 teaspoon vanilla extract
1 1/4 cups fine-grated coconut
1 unbaked 9-inch pie shell

Preheat oven to 425°.

Beat together the eggs, salt and sugar. Stir in the milk, cream and vanilla, then the coconut. Pour into the lined pie plate. Bake 30 minutes or until a knife inserted in the center comes out clean. Cool on a cake rack.

Fruit Custard-Meringue Pie

FILLING

Pastry for 1-crust pie
2 cups peeled sliced apples or peaches
3 egg yolks
1/8 teaspoon salt
2/3 cup sugar
2 cups milk
1/2 teaspoon vanilla extract

Preheat oven to 450°. Line a 9-inch pie plate with the pastry. Chill 10 minutes.

Arrange the fruit on the bottom of the lined pie plate. Beat the egg yolks, salt and sugar until light and fluffy. Mix in the milk and vanilla; pour over the fruit. Bake 10 minutes; reduce heat to 325° and bake 30 minutes longer or until a knife inserted in the center comes out clean. Cool.

MERINGUE

3 egg whites
1/3 cup sugar
3 tablespoons finely chopped nuts

Preheat oven to 425°.

Beat the egg whites until soft peaks are formed, then gradually beat in the sugar until stiff. Fold in the nuts. Spread over the pie, covering the edges. Bake 5 minutes or until delicately browned. Cool.

Orange-Custard Pie

4 eggs
¾ cup sugar
1½ cups light cream, scalded
2 teaspoons grated orange rind
1⅔ cups orange juice
1 9-inch unbaked pie shell
2 oranges, peeled, seeded and sectioned
1½ teaspoons cornstarch
3 tablespoons orange liqueur (Curaçao)

Preheat oven to 425°.

Beat the eggs and sugar until light and fluffy; gradually beat in the cream. Mix in the orange rind and 1⅓ cups orange juice. Pour into the lined pie plate. Bake 35 minutes or until a knife inserted in the center comes out clean. Arrange the orange sections on top.

In a small saucepan, mix together the cornstarch and remaining orange juice. Cook over low heat, stirring steadily until thick and clear. Add the liqueur. Spoon evenly over the oranges. Chill.

Banana Pie

Pastry for 2-crust pie
6 bananas
½ cup sugar
1 tablespoon melted butter
½ cup ground almonds
1 cup chopped seedless raisins
1 teaspoon cinnamon
¼ teaspoon nutmeg
½ teaspoon powdered ginger
3 egg whites, stiffly beaten

Preheat oven to 425°.

Line a 9-inch pie plate with a little more than half the pastry. Chill while preparing the filling.

Mash the bananas until very smooth. Stir in the sugar, butter, almonds, raisins, cinnamon, nutmeg and ginger. Fold in the egg whites. Turn the banana mixture into the lined pie plate. Cover with the remaining rolled-out pastry. Bake 35 minutes or until browned. Cool on a cake rack.

Serves 6–8.

Lemon-Curd Meringue Pie

3 eggs
1⅛ cups sugar
⅓ cup lemon juice
6 tablespoons butter
1 tablespoon grated lemon rind
Baked 9-inch pastry shell
3 egg whites

Preheat oven to 400°.

Beat the eggs and ⅞ cup of the sugar in the top of a double boiler. Stir in the lemon juice and add the butter, broken into small pieces. Place over hot water and cook, stirring steadily until thickened and mixture coats the spoon. Stir in the lemon rind and let cool. Pour into the pie plate.

Beat the egg whites until peaks form, then beat in the remaining sugar, a tablespoon at a time, until stiff but not dry. Heap on the lemon filling (using a pastry tube, if you like). Bake 5 minutes or until meringue is delicately browned. Cool.

Lemon Sponge Pie

1¼ cups crushed vanilla wafers
3 tablespoons melted butter
¼ pound (1 stick) butter
¾ cup sugar
2 tablespoons cornstarch
3 egg yolks
1 cup milk
3 tablespoons lemon juice
2 teaspoons grated lemon rind
3 egg whites, stiffly beaten

Preheat oven to 350°.

Mix the vanilla wafers and melted butter together. Line a 9-inch buttered pie plate with the mixture. Chill while preparing the filling.

Cream the ¼ pound butter, gradually adding the sugar and cornstarch. Beat until light and fluffy. Add 1 egg yolk at a time, beating after each addition. Add the milk, lemon juice and rind, beating very well. Fold in the egg whites carefully but thoroughly. Pour into prepared pie plate. Bake 35 minutes or until delicately browned.

Lemon Chiffon Pie

1 envelope (tablespoon) gelatin
¼ cup cold water
4 egg yolks
1 cup sugar
½ cup lemon juice
1 teaspoon grated lemon rind
2 egg whites
⅛ teaspoon salt
½ cup heavy cream
9-inch baked pastry or crumb shell

Soften the gelatin in the water. Beat the egg yolks in the top of a double boiler; mix in ½ cup sugar and the lemon juice. Place over hot water and cook, stirring steadily, until mixture coats the spoon. Mix in the gelatin until dissolved, then the rind. Remove from the hot water and let cool, mixing occasionally.

Beat the egg whites and salt until they begin to stiffen, then gradually beat in the remaining sugar until stiff. Whip the cream. Fold in the lemon mixture, then the beaten egg whites. Turn into the prepared pie shell. Chill until set. Decorate with whipped cream if you like.

VARIATION

Lime Chiffon Pie: Substitute lime juice and rind for the lemon and add 2 drops of green food coloring.

Mocha Chiffon Pie

1 envelope (tablespoon) gelatin
¼ cup cold water
1 cup milk
1 cup semi-sweet chocolate chips
1 tablespoon instant coffee
¼ teaspoon salt
2 egg yolks
½ cup heavy cream
2 egg whites
3 tablespoons sugar
9-inch baked pastry or crumb shell

Soften the gelatin in the water. In a saucepan, combine the milk, chocolate, coffee and salt. Cook over low heat, stirring steadily until chocolate melts. Beat the egg yolks in a bowl; very gradually add the chocolate mixture, stirring steadily to prevent curdling. Return to the saucepan and cook, stirring steadily until thickened. Do not let boil. Remove from the heat and stir in the gelatin until dissolved. Cool. Whip the cream. Beat the egg whites until foamy; gradually beat in the sugar until stiff. Fold into the chocolate mixture with the whipped cream. Turn into the pie shell. Chill until firm. Decorate with whipped cream and shaved chocolate if desired.

Italian Fruit-Almond Pie

PASTRY

1¼ cups flour
½ teaspoon salt
1 teaspoon baking powder
¼ cup sugar
½ teaspoon cinnamon
2 teaspoons grated lemon rind
¼ pound (1 stick) butter or margarine
2 egg yolks
2 tablespoons Marsala or sweet sherry

Sift the flour, salt, baking powder, sugar, cinnamon and lemon rind into a bowl. Cut in the butter with a pastry blender or 2 knives. Beat the egg yolks and wine; stir into the flour mixture with a fork until all the particles hold together. Roll out on a lightly floured surface to fit an 11-inch pie plate. Fit the dough into the greased pie plate. Chill while preparing the filling.

FILLING

5 cups sliced apples
2 tablespoons cognac
¾ cup sugar
2 tablespoons flour
½ cup ground almonds
½ teaspoon cinnamon
¼ teaspoon mace

Preheat oven to 375°.

Toss the apples with the cognac; arrange in the lined pie plate. Mix together the sugar, flour, nuts, cinnamon and mace; sprinkle over the apples. Bake 45 minutes or until apples are tender. Serve warm or cold, cut into wedges.

Boston Cream Pie

CAKE

1¾ cups sifted cake flour
¼ teaspoon salt
2 teaspoons baking powder
6 tablespoons butter
1 cup sugar
1 teaspoon vanilla extract
2 egg yolks
½ cup milk
2 egg whites, beaten stiff

Preheat oven to 375°.

Sift together the flour, salt and baking powder. Cream the butter; gradually beat in the sugar until very fluffy. Beat in the vanilla, then 1 egg yolk at a time. Add the flour and milk alternately, stirring only until blended. Start and end with the flour. Fold in the egg whites carefully but thoroughly. Turn into a greased 9-inch pie plate. Bake 35 minutes or until a cake tester comes out clean. Cool on a cake rack 10 minutes, then remove from the pie plate. Turn right side up. With a sharp knife, cut out about a 7-inch circle almost down to the bottom. Lift up carefully. Fill the cake, and replace top. Cover with Chocolate Glaze.

FILLING

½ cup flour
⅔ cup sugar
⅛ teaspoon salt
2 cups milk, scalded
2 egg yolks
1 teaspoon vanilla extract
1 cup whipped cream

Sift the flour, sugar and salt into the top of a double boiler. Stir in the hot milk gradually. Place over hot water and cook, stirring constantly, until thickened. Cook 5 minutes longer.

Beat the egg yolks in a bowl; gradually add the hot mixture, stirring steadily to prevent curdling. Return to the double boiler and cook 2 minutes, stirring steadily. Cool. Stir in the vanilla and fold in the whipped cream.

Pumpkin Pie

Pastry for 1-crust pie
2 cups cooked or canned pumpkin
½ teaspoon salt
⅔ cup firmly packed brown sugar
1 teaspoon cinnamon
½ teaspoon ground ginger
½ teaspoon nutmeg
2 eggs, beaten
1 cup milk
1 cup light cream
2 tablespoons cognac

Preheat oven to 325°. Line a 9-inch pie plate with the pastry and chill while preparing the filling.

Using an electric blender, electric mixer or rotary beater, beat together the pumpkin, salt, brown sugar, cinnamon, ginger, nutmeg and eggs until smooth, then gradually add the milk, cream and cognac. Pour into the lined pie plate. Bake 50 minutes or until a knife inserted in the center comes out clean. Serve warm, with whipped cream if desired.

Frozen Eggnog Pie

1½ cups graham cracker crumbs
⅓ cup ground unblanched almonds
⅓ cup confectioners' sugar
¼ cup light cream
½ cup melted butter
1 envelope (tablespoon) gelatin
1 cup milk
¾ cup granulated sugar
¼ teaspoon salt
4 egg yolks
2 tablespoons cognac or light rum
4 egg whites
¼ cup sliced candied cherries

Preheat the oven to 375°.

Mix together the cracker crumbs, almonds, confectioners' sugar, cream and butter. Press the mixture into a 9-inch pie plate. Bake 15 minutes. Cool and chill.

Soften the gelatin in the milk in the top of a double boiler. Add ¼ cup of the granulated sugar, the salt and egg yolks. Beat until blended. Place over hot water and cook, stirring constantly until thickened and the mixture coats the back of the spoon. Remove from the heat, mix in the cognac and chill until thickened but not firm.

Beat the egg whites until foamy. Gradually add the remaining half cup of sugar, beating until stiff but not dry. Fold the meringue and the cherries into the gelatin mixture. Pile in the crumb shell. Cover with clear plastic wrap supported above the filling on four to six toothpicks stuck into the pie. Freeze, then wrap in foil. To serve the pie, thaw it at room temperature one hour. Decorate with whipped cream and cherries if desired.

Makes 6 servings.

Black Bottom Pie

2 cups gingersnap crumbs
½ cup (¼ pound) melted butter
1 envelope (tablespoon) gelatin
¼ cup cold water
4 egg yolks
1½ tablespoons cornstarch
¾ cup sugar
2 cups milk, scalded
2 squares (ounces) unsweetened chocolate, melted
1 teaspoon vanilla extract
3 tablespoons rum
4 egg whites
1 cup heavy cream
Shaved chocolate

Preheat oven to 350°.

Mix the crumbs and melted butter together. Press onto the sides and bottom of an 11-inch buttered pie plate. Bake 10 minutes; cool.

Soften the gelatin in the water. In the top of a double boiler, beat the egg yolks, cornstarch and ½ cup sugar; gradually add the hot milk, mixing steadily. Place over hot water and cook, mixing steadily until mixture coats the spoon. Remove from heat and pour half the mixture into a bowl; mix in the chocolate and vanilla. Cool, then pour into the pie shell. To mixture remaining in the double boiler, add the gelatin and rum, stirring until gelatin dissolves. Cool. Beat the egg whites until soft peaks are formed; gradually beat in the remaining sugar until stiff. Whip the cream and fold half into the gelatin mixture with the beaten egg whites. Pour into the pie plate. Chill. Cover top with the remaining whipped cream and shaved chocolate.

Black Walnut Pie

2 tablespoons flour
¼ cup sugar
2 eggs
1 cup dark corn syrup
½ cup water
1 cup (¼ pound) black walnuts
1 unbaked 9-inch pastry shell

Preheat the oven to 375°.

Mix the flour and sugar. Beat the eggs, then beat in the sugar mixture until blended. Stir in the corn syrup and water. Mix in the nuts. Pour into pastry shell. Bake 35 minutes or until a knife inserted in the center comes out clean.

Pecan Pie

Pastry for 1-crust pie
4 tablespoons butter
⅔ cup firmly packed dark brown sugar
¾ cup dark corn syrup
3 eggs
1 teaspoon vanilla extract
1 cup pecan halves

Preheat oven to 400°. Line an 8-inch pie plate with the pastry; chill while preparing the filling.

Cream the butter, gradually beating in the brown sugar until light and fluffy. Beat in the corn syrup, then 1 egg at a time. Mix in the vanilla and pecans. Turn into the lined pie plate. Bake 10 minutes; reduce heat to 350° and bake 30 minutes longer or until a knife inserted in the center comes out clean. Cool. Serve with whipped cream if desired.

Cheese Pie

1 pound cream cheese
¾ cup sugar
2 eggs
2 tablespoons heavy cream
2 teaspoons vanilla extract
9-inch pie plate, lined with pastry dough or graham cracker pastry
½ cup sour cream

Preheat oven to 350°.

Using an electric mixer or rotary beater, beat the cheese until smooth. Add all but 2 tablespoons sugar; beat until light and fluffy. Beat in the eggs, cream and 1 teaspoon vanilla. Turn into the lined pie plate. Bake 20 minutes.

Mix together the sour cream and remaining vanilla and sugar. Spread over the top of the pie at the end of 20 minutes' baking time. Raise heat to 425° and bake 5 minutes longer. Cool, then chill several hours before serving.

Crustless Fudge Pie

2 squares (ounces) unsweetened chocolate
2 tablespoons brewed coffee
¼ pound (1 stick) butter or margarine
1 cup sugar
⅛ teaspoon salt
1 teaspoon vanilla
2 egg yolks
⅓ cup sifted flour
2 egg whites, stiffly beaten

Preheat oven to 350°.

Melt the chocolate in the coffee; cool. Cream the butter, gradually adding the sugar. Beat until light and fluffy. Add the salt, vanilla and 1 egg yolk at a time. Add the flour and chocolate, mixing thoroughly. Fold in the egg whites carefully.

Pour into a buttered 9-inch pie plate. Bake 45 minutes or until set and puffed. Cool and serve with whipped cream. Cut like a pie.

Vanilla Cream Pie

⅔ cup sugar
½ teaspoon salt
3 tablespoons cornstarch
2½ cups milk
3 egg yolks
2 tablespoons butter or margarine
2 teaspoons vanilla extract
1 9-inch baked pastry or crumb shell

In the top of a double boiler, mix the sugar, salt and cornstarch. Stir in the milk. Cook over low heat, stirring constantly to the boiling point, then cook 3 minutes longer. Beat the egg yolks in a bowl; gradually add the hot mixture, stirring steadily to prevent curdling. Return to the double boiler and place over boiling water. Cook 10 minutes, stirring frequently. Remove from the heat and stir in the butter and vanilla until butter melts. Cool. Pour into the pie shell and chill. Cover with whipped cream and shaved chocolate if desired.

VARIATION

Chocolate Cream Pie: Add 2 squares (ounces) melted semi-sweet chocolate to the mixture when adding the butter.

Coconut Meringue-Shell Pie

¼ pound sweet chocolate
3 tablespoons brewed coffee
2 egg yolks, beaten
1 cup heavy cream
1 tablespoon confectioners' sugar
1 9-inch baked Coconut Meringue Shell

Break the chocolate into small pieces; combine with the coffee in a small saucepan. Place over hot water until melted; stir until smooth. Cool 5 minutes. Gradually add the egg yolks, stirring constantly to prevent curdling. Return to the hot water and cook 1 minute, mixing steadily. Cool. Whip the cream and confectioners' sugar. Fold half into the chocolate mixture. Spread remaining whipped cream on the bottom of the pie shell. Cover with the chocolate mixture. Chill at least 4 hours. Decorate with whipped cream if desired.

Sweet Potato-Nut Pie

Pastry for 1-crust pie
4 eggs
½ teaspoon salt
½ cup sugar
1½ cups mashed sweet potatoes
2 tablespoons honey
⅔ cup milk
⅓ cup orange juice
1 teaspoon vanilla extract
¼ teaspoon nutmeg
½ cup chopped walnuts or pecans

Preheat oven to 375°. Line a 9-inch pie plate with the pastry and chill while preparing the filling.

Beat the eggs and salt, then beat in the sugar. Beat in the sweet potatoes and honey until smooth. Add the milk, orange juice, vanilla and nutmeg, beating again until smooth. Stir in the nuts. Pour into the lined pie plate. Bake 40 minutes or until a knife inserted in the center comes out clean. Serve warm, with whipped cream if desired.

Tarts

Fruit Cream Tart, Paris Fashion

3 tablespoons cornstarch
⅛ teaspoon salt
1¼ cups sugar
1 cup light cream
1 cup milk, scalded
3 egg yolks
1 teaspoon vanilla extract
½ cup heavy cream, whipped
9-inch baked French Tart Paste shell
½ cup water
1 teaspoon lemon juice
2 cups sliced peaches, blueberries, black cherries or halved apricots

In the top of a double boiler, mix the cornstarch, salt and ¼ cup sugar. Mix in the cream, then the hot milk. Place over hot water and cook, stirring steadily until thickened; cook 10 minutes longer, stirring occasionally. Beat the egg yolks in a bowl; gradually add the hot sauce, stirring steadily to prevent curdling. Return to top of double boiler; cook 2 minutes, stirring steadily, but do not let boil. Remove from heat, mix in the vanilla and cool. Fold in the cream and pour into the baked tart shell. Cook the remaining sugar, the water and lemon juice 5 minutes. Add the selected fruit; cook 5 minutes. Remove the fruit with a slotted spoon and cool. Cook the syrup 10 minutes or until very thick. Cool 10 minutes. Arrange the fruit over the cream mixture and brush with the syrup. Cool.

Peach Tart

Pastry for 1-crust pie
1 tablespoon melted butter
3 cups sliced peaches
½ cup sugar
½ teaspoon cinnamon
1 egg yolk
¼ cup heavy cream

Preheat oven to 375°.

Line a 9-inch pie plate with the pastry and brush bottom with the butter. Arrange the peaches in it; sprinkle with the sugar mixed with the cinnamon. Bake 20 minutes. Beat together the egg yolk and cream; pour over the fruit. Baked 15 minutes longer or until fruit is tender. Cool on a cake rack.

French Lemon Tart

2 eggs
½ cup sugar
⅓ cup lemon juice
¾ cup ground blanched almonds
2 teaspoons grated lemon rind
¼ teaspoon almond extract
8-inch French Tart Pastry-lined pie plate, baked 10 minutes and cooled

Preheat oven to 325°. Place oven rack on middle level.

Beat the eggs and sugar until very thick and light. Beat in the lemon juice, almonds, lemon rind and almond extract. Turn into the pastry shell. Bake 25 minutes or until a knife inserted in the center comes out clean. Cool on a cake rack.

Cherry Tart, Normandy Fashion

1½ pounds black cherries
9-inch unbaked French Tart Paste shell
½ cup sugar
1 teaspoon lemon juice
⅛ teaspoon almond extract
½ cup currant jelly
2 tablespoons water

Preheat oven to 375°.

Pit the cherries and arrange in the tart shell. Sprinkle with the sugar, lemon juice and almond extract. Bake 30 minutes or until browned and cherries tender. Cool.

Melt the jelly with the water and brush over the cherries until evenly glazed. Cool and decorate with whipped cream if desired.

Individual French Fruit Tarts

(FEUILLETÉS AUX FRUITS DIVERS)

Puff Paste Recipe
Egg yolks
Apricots and/or plums
Apricot jam

Preheat oven to 425°.

Make as many or as few tarts as you like. Roll out the pastry ¼-inch thick and fit into tart pans. Brush with the beaten yolks and place a halved apricot or plum, cut side up on each. Bake 20 minutes or until fruit is tender but firm. Immediately brush with melted apricot jam to glaze fruit.

Caramelized Apple Tart

(TARTE TATIN)

PASTRY

1 cup sifted flour
⅛ teaspoon salt
¼ cup sugar
¼ pound butter
3 tablespoons ice water

FILLING

6 tablespoons butter
½ cup sugar
3 cups peeled, sliced apples

Sift the flour, salt and sugar into a bowl; cut in the butter with a pastry blender or 2 knives. Add the water and toss lightly until a ball of dough is formed. Chill 1 hour.

Use a deep 9-inch pie plate and butter it with 2 tablespoons of the butter. Sprinkle with 3 tablespoons of the sugar. Arrange the apples in layers; dot with the remaining butter and sprinkle with 3 tablespoons sugar. Roll out the pastry and cover the apples with it. Bake in a preheated 375° oven 30 minutes. Cool 5 minutes, then carefully invert onto a serving plate so that the pastry is now underneath with the apples on top. Sprinkle with the remaining sugar and place under the broiler until sugar browns. Cool.

Cheese Tart

¼ pound (1 stick) sweet butter
½ pound cream cheese
⅔ cup sugar
2 eggs
⅛ teaspoon nutmeg
8-inch French Tart Pastry-lined pie plate, baked 10 minutes and cooled

Preheat oven to 375°. Place oven rack on middle level.

Cream the butter with an electric mixer or wooden spoon. Beat in the cheese and sugar until very smooth, then the eggs and nutmeg. Be sure the mixture is smooth and light. Turn into the pastry shell. Bake 25 minutes or until a knife inserted in the center comes out clean. Serve hot, or cool on a cake rack. Don't worry if center sinks slightly.

Nut Tart

4 egg yolks
2 cups sugar
2 cups ground toasted filberts (hazel nuts)
2 teaspoons vanilla extract
Pastry for 2-crust pie

Preheat the oven to 400°.

Beat the egg yolks, gradually adding the sugar. Beat until thick and smooth. Stir in the nuts and vanilla.

Line a 9-inch pie plate with half the pastry and fill with the nut mixture. Cover with the remaining pastry, sealing the edges well. Bake 35 minutes or until browned. Cool.

Nut Custard Tart

1 cup ground walnuts or pecans
9-inch pastry-lined pie shell
5 eggs
⅔ cup sugar
2 cups light cream
1 teaspoon vanilla extract
½ cup currant jelly
1 tablespoon cognac

Press nuts into the bottom of the pastry. Chill in the freezing compartment of refrigerator or home freezer 1½ hours.

Beat the eggs and sugar until thick and light. Mix in the cream and vanilla. Pour into the pie shell. Bake in a preheated 350° oven, with rack on lowest level, 50 minutes or until a knife inserted in the center comes out clean.

While pie is baking, melt the jelly; stir in the cognac. Brush over the top of the pie immediately upon removing from oven. Cool on a cake rack, then chill.

French Almond Paste Tart

(PITHIVIER)

¼ pound butter
½ cup sugar
1 cup blanched ground almonds
3 eggs
¼ cup sifted flour
Puff Paste recipe
1 egg yolk
Confectioners' sugar

Preheat oven to 400°.

Cream the butter, gradually adding the sugar. Beat until creamy and light. Beat in the almonds and 1 egg at a time. Sift in the flour and mix until absorbed.

Roll out the pastry ⅛ inch thick and cut into three 8-inch circles. Brush with beaten egg yolk, then spread the almond mixture on two circles, leaving ½-inch border all around. Put the two together, spread side up and cover with the remaining circle. Press edges together gently. Bake until browned, about 35 minutes. Five minutes before baking time is up, sprinkle with confectioners' sugar.

Spanish Almond Tarts

PASTRY SHELLS

2 cups sifted flour
½ teaspoon salt
¼ cup confectioners' sugar
½ pound (2 sticks) butter
1 egg, beaten
¼ cup ice water

Sift the flour, salt and sugar into a bowl. Work in the butter with the hand; then blend the egg. Add just enough of the water to make a dough. Chill 2 hours. Roll out ¼ inch thick on a lightly floured surface and fit into twelve tart or muffin tins. Reserve pieces of pastry for tops. Preheat the oven to 425°.

FILLING

¼ pound (1 stick) butter
½ cup sugar
4 eggs
1 cup ground almonds
2 tablespoons cognac
1 teaspoon almond extract

Cream the butter and sugar until fluffy. Beat in the eggs; then stir in the almonds, cognac and almond extract. Spoon into the pastry shells. Roll out the remaining pastry very thin and cut into narrow strips. Place over the filling in a crisscross fashion. Bake 20 minutes or until browned and set. Cool and remove from pan.

Fried Desserts

French Crullers

1 cup water
¼ pound (1 stick) butter
½ teaspoon salt
1 teaspoon sugar
1 cup sifted flour
4 eggs
2 teaspoons vanilla extract
Vegetable oil for deep frying
Confectioners' sugar

Combine the water, butter, salt and sugar in a saucepan. Bring to a boil, and when butter melts, add the flour all at once. Beat with a wooden spoon until mixture forms a ball and leaves the sides of the pan. Remove from the heat.

Separate 2 of the eggs. Add 1 whole egg at a time, then 1 egg yolk at a time, beating after each addition until smooth and shiny. Stir in the vanilla. Cool. Beat the 2 egg whites until stiff and fold into the paste.

Use a pastry bag with a star tube, or use a spoon, and shape the mixture into 2-inch rings on a piece of buttered aluminum foil or waxed paper.

Heat the oil to 370°. Invert the paper over the pan and drop the rings into it. Don't crowd the crullers in the pan. Fry until browned. Drain, sprinkle with confectioners' sugar and serve hot.

Makes about 12.

Italian Crullers

(SFINGE)

2 cups sifted flour
¼ teaspoon salt
3 teaspoons baking powder
½ teaspoon mace
2 eggs
½ cup sugar
1 tablespoon vegetable oil
⅓ cup milk
Vegetable oil for deep frying
Powdered sugar

Sift together the flour, salt, baking powder and mace. Beat the eggs, sugar and oil until thick. Stir in the milk, then the flour mixture. Beat until very smooth. Cover with a towel and let stand 15 minutes.

Heat the fat to 370°. Drop the batter into it by the tablespoon, a few at a time. Fry until browned, about 4 minutes. Remove with a slotted spoon and drain. Sprinkle with sugar, anise-flavored if you like.

Makes about 3 dozen.

New Orleans Doughnuts

(CROQUIGNOLES)

¾ cup warm water
2 tablespoons vegetable oil
⅓ cup sugar
½ teaspoon salt
½ cup evaporated milk
1 package yeast
4 cups sifted flour (approximately)
2 eggs, beaten
Vegetable oil for deep frying
Confectioners' sugar

In a bowl combine ½ cup of the warm water, the oil, sugar, salt and evaporated milk. Sprinkle the yeast into the remaining water. Stir until dissolved. Add to the previous mixture. Stir in the flour and eggs alternately, beating hard and briskly. If necessary, add more flour to make a soft dough. Turn dough out on a lightly-floured board and knead gently until smooth and elastic. Place dough in an oiled bowl and brush top lightly with oil; cover with a clean cloth and let rise in a warm place 30 minutes.

Punch dough down and turn out onto a lightly-floured board. Divide dough in half. Keep unused portion of dough covered. Roll half the dough at a time into a rectangle about ½-inch thick. Cut into small triangles or into rectangles about 1½ by 1 inch. Stretch the dough with the fingers until double in size and thin. Pieces should be slightly thinner in center. Heat the oil to 375°. Fry a few doughnuts at a time in a single layer, without crowding, until browned. Turn to cook and brown all sides evenly. Drain on absorbent paper. Dust with confectioners' sugar. Serve hot.

Makes about 4 dozen.

Middle East Crullers

½ cup water
⅛ teaspoon salt
¼ pound (1 stick) butter
⅔ cup sifted flour
3 eggs
3 tablespoons currants or seedless raisins
2 tablespoons finely chopped candied fruits
1 tablespoon rose water
Vegetable oil for deep frying
Confectioners' sugar

Combine the water, salt and butter in a saucepan. Bring to a boil and cook until butter melts. Add the flour all at once, beating vigorously with a wooden spoon until mixture forms a ball and leaves the sides of the pan. Remove from the heat and add 1 egg at a time, beating until smooth and glossy after each addition. Beat in the currants, candied fruits and rose water.

Heat the oil to 370°. Drop the paste into it by the teaspoon. Leave enough space in the pan for crullers to turn themselves. Fry until browned on all sides. Drain and sprinkle with confectioners' sugar. Serve hot or cold.

Makes about 24.

Note: Rose water is obtainable in specialty food shops or drug stores.

Parisian Fried Puffs

(BEIGNETS SOUFFLÉS)

1 cup water
¼ teaspoon salt
¼ pound (1 stick) butter
1 cup sifted flour
4 eggs
1 tablespoon cognac
Vegetable oil for deep frying
Confectioners' sugar

Combine the water, salt and butter in a saucepan. Bring to a boil and cook until butter melts. Add the flour all at once, beating vigorously with a wooden spoon until mixture forms a ball and leaves the sides of the pan. Remove from the heat. Cool slightly, then add 1 egg at a time, beating after each addition until smooth and glossy. Beat in the cognac.

Heat the oil to 370°. Drop the paste into it by the scant tablespoon. Allow enough space for *beignets* to turn themselves. Fry until browned on all sides. Drain and sprinkle with confectioners' sugar. The *beignets* may also be filled with jelly if you like. Make a small hole in the side and fill.

Makes about 16.

South American Crullers

(BUÑUELOS)

SYRUP

2 tablespoons cornstarch
1 cup water
1 cup firmly packed dark brown sugar
2 tablespoons butter
2 tablespoons heavy cream
1 teaspoon vanilla extract

Mix the cornstarch and water in a saucepan until smooth; stir in the brown sugar. Bring to a boil, cook over low heat, stirring constantly; then cook until thick, about 10 minutes, stirring occasionally. Mix in the butter, cream and vanilla. Keep warm while preparing the crullers.

CRULLERS

1 cup water
½ cup sugar
3 tablespoons butter
2 tablespoons grated lemon rind
1 cup sifted cake flour
3 eggs
Vegetable oil for deep frying

In a saucepan, combine the water, sugar, butter and lemon rind. Bring to a boil, and when butter melts, add the flour all at once, mixing with a wooden spoon until the dough leaves the sides of the pan and forms a ball. Cool 5 minutes. Add 1 egg at a time, beating until shiny and smooth after each addition.

Heat the oil to 375°. Drop the batter into it by the teaspoon. Don't crowd the pan. Fry until browned on both sides. Drain. Heap crullers in a bowl and pour the hot syrup over them.

Serves 6–8.

Indian Crullers

(JALEBI)

1 package yeast
2 cups warm water
½ teaspoon saffron
2¾ cups sifted flour
Vegetable oil for deep frying
2 cups light corn syrup

Soften the yeast in ¼ cup of the warm water. Dissolve the saffron in the remaining water.

Sift the flour into a bowl; beat in the yeast mixture and saffron water until very smooth.

Heat the oil to 375°. Use a funnel with a small opening and pour the batter through it into the hot oil. Move the funnel in circles, to make spirals. Don't crowd the crullers in the pan. Fry until golden brown on both sides.

Heat the syrup, but don't boil. Dip the fried crullers in the hot syrup, coating both sides. Drain. Serve hot or cold.

Serves 8–10.

Buttermilk Doughnuts

2¼ cups sifted flour
¾ teaspoon salt
¾ teaspoon baking soda
¾ teaspoon cream of tartar
¼ teaspoon nutmeg
1 egg
1 egg yolk
½ cup sugar
1½ tablespoons vegetable oil
½ cup buttermilk
Vegetable oil for deep frying

Sift together the flour, salt, baking soda, cream of tartar and nutmeg. Beat the egg and egg yolk in a large bowl until thick, then gradually beat in the sugar until light. Mix in the oil and buttermilk, then add the flour mixture. Stir until well blended. Chill 1 hour.

Roll out the dough ¼-inch thick on a well-floured surface. Cut with a 3-inch floured doughnut cutter. Try not to handle the dough too much.

Heat the oil to 375°. Fry a few doughnuts at a time until browned on both sides. Drain. Sprinkle with confectioners' sugar if desired.

Makes about 18.

Fried Puffs

(BRANDKRAPFEN)

¼ pound (1 stick) butter
1 cup milk
¼ teaspoon salt
3 tablespoon granulated sugar
1 cup sifted flour
1 teaspoon grated lemon rind
4 eggs
Vegetable oil for deep frying
¼ cup powdered sugar
½ teaspoon vanilla powder

Combine the butter, milk, salt and the granulated sugar in a saucepan. Bring to a boil, and when butter is melted, add the flour all at once, stirring with a wooden spoon until mixture forms a ball and leaves the sides of the pan. Remove from the heat and beat in the lemon rind. Let stand 5 minutes, then add 1 egg at a time, beating after each addition until smooth.

Heat the oil to 370°. Use 2 teaspoons to shape 1-inch balls of the mixture. Fry until delicately browned on all sides. Leave enough space in the pan so the balls can turn by themselves. Drain and sprinkle with the powdered sugar mixed with the vanilla powder. Serve hot.

Makes about 32.

Apple Fritters

(BEIGNETS DE POMMES)

2 cups sifted flour
½ teaspoon salt
2 eggs, separated
1 teaspoon cognac
1 cup milk
4 cooking apples, peeled, cored and sliced into ⅛-inch-thick rounds
Fat for deep frying
Powdered sugar

Sift the flour into a bowl. Make a well in the center and put in it the salt, egg yolks and cognac. Work in the flour from sides to center until thoroughly mixed. Slowly add the milk, beating with a whisk until the batter is smooth. Beat the egg whites until stiff and fold in. Dip the apple rounds in the batter and fry in 375° deep fat until delicately browned. Sprinkle with powdered sugar and serve.

Serves 4.

Venezuelan Banana Fritters

4 bananas
4 egg yolks, beaten
3 egg whites, stiffly beaten
1½ teaspoons baking powder
⅓ cup vegetable oil
½ cup powdered sugar

Buy very ripe bananas; mash smooth. Mix in the egg yolks, then fold in the egg whites and baking powder. Heat the oil in a skillet until it bubbles. Drop the mixture into it by the tablespoon. Brown the patties on both sides. Drain, dip in the sugar, and serve hot.

Serves 4–6.

Viennese Fritters

(ZUCKERSTRAUBEN)

¼ cup sugar
⅔ cup flour
½ teaspoon salt
½ cup white wine (approximately)
6 egg whites, stiffly beaten
Vegetable oil for deep frying
Confectioners' sugar

Sift the sugar, flour and salt into a bowl. Beat in just enough of the wine to make a medium-thick batter. Fold in the beaten egg whites.

Heat the oil to 370°. Use a pastry bag with a fluted tube. Put the mixture through it in 1½-inch lengths (or drop by the tablespoon). Don't crowd the fritters in the pan. Fry until delicately browned. Drain, sprinkle with confectioners' sugar and serve with Sabayon Sauce or Foamy Sauce.

Serves 8–10.

Fruit Fritters

COGNAC BATTER

¾ cup sifted flour
⅛ teaspoon salt
1 tablespoon sugar
3 tablespoons warm water
3 tablespoons cognac
1 tablespoon melted butter
1 egg yolk, beaten
1 egg white, beaten stiff

Sift the flour, salt and sugar into a bowl. Mix in the water and cognac until smooth, then beat in the butter and egg yolk. The batter should look like heavy cream, so, if necessary, add a little more flour or water to obtain that result. Fold in the egg white. Dip the selected fruit (if large) in the batter, and fry a few at a time in deep 370° fat until browned. (If berries are used, add 2 cups sugared, drained berries to the batter.) Drop by the tablespoon into the fat and fry until browned. Drain, arrange in a shallow baking pan, sprinkle with granulated sugar and set under the broiler until sugar is glazed. Serve with confectioners' sugar or a sauce.

Serves 4–6.

APPLE FRITTERS

3 apples
¼ cup sugar
½ teaspoon cinnamon
2 teaspoons cognac

Peel, core and slice the apples very thin. Sprinkle with the sugar, cinnamon and cognac. Cover and let stand 1 hour. Drain and proceed as directed above.

Hungarian Batter-Fried Cherries

(CZERESZNYE KISUTVE)

1 pound sweet cherries
1 cup sifted flour
¼ cup sugar
½ cup milk
⅓ cup sweet sherry
2 eggs, beaten
Vegetable oil for deep frying
½ cup sifted confectioners' sugar
1 teaspoon cinnamon

Try to buy cherries in clusters, and be sure they're firm. Wash and dry.

Sift the flour and sugar into a bowl. Beat in the milk, sherry and eggs until very smooth. Dip the cherries in the batter, coating them well.

Heat the oil to 370°. Fry the cherries in it until browned. Drain and sprinkle with a mixture of the confectioners' sugar and cinnamon.

Serves 6–8.

BERRY FRITTERS

2 cups blueberries, raspberries or halved strawberries
⅓ cup sugar
2 teaspoons cognac

Wash and dry the berries. Sprinkle with the sugar and cognac. Cover and let stand 30 minutes. Drain well and proceed as directed above.

BANANA FRITTERS

4 bananas
¼ cup sugar
2 teaspoons lemon juice
2 teaspoons cognac

Peel the bananas; cut in half crosswise, then in half lengthwise. Sprinkle with the sugar, lemon juice and cognac. Cover and let stand 30 minutes. Turn pieces a few times. Drain and proceed as directed above.

Pancakes and Crêpes

French Pancakes

(CRÊPES)

3 eggs
1/8 teaspoon salt
1 1/2 cups milk
1 1/8 cups sifted flour
2 tablespoons vegetable oil
Butter

Sift the flour into a bowl. Beat the eggs, salt and milk together; add to the flour, stirring until smooth. Mix in the oil. Chill 1 hour. The batter should have the consistency of heavy cream; add more flour or milk if necessary.

Melt a little butter in a 6-inch skillet until it sizzles. Pour enough batter into it to just cover the bottom (about 2 tablespoons), tilting the pan as you pour. Bake until delicately browned on both sides. Stack the pancakes while preparing the balance if they are to be filled. If not, fold into quarters or roll up.

Makes about 24.

Cottage Cheese Pancakes

2 cups cottage cheese, drained
2 teaspoons sugar
½ teaspoon salt
1 egg, beaten
1 cup bread crumbs
½ cup sifted flour
¼ pound butter

Combine the cheese, sugar, salt and egg. Beat well. Add the bread crumbs, mixing until well blended. Form heaping tablespoons of the mixture into pancakes. Dip in the flour.

Melt half the butter in a skillet. Bake the pancakes in it until browned on both sides, adding more butter as necessary. Serve hot, dusted with sugar, preserves or stewed fruit.

Makes about 24.

Pancakes in Orange Sauce

(CRÊPES SUZETTE)

¼ pound (1 stick) sweet butter
⅓ cup sugar
½ cup orange juice
2 tablespoons grated orange rind
1 teaspoon lemon juice
⅓ cup Cointreau or Curaçao
Crêpes recipe
¼ cup warm cognac

Cream the butter, sugar, orange juice and rind and lemon juice until light and fluffy. Heat the mixture in the flat pan of a chafing dish or an electric skillet, if you wish to prepare it at the table. Otherwise, use an ordinary skillet. Fold the crêpes in quarters and place in the mixture; turn over to heat and moisten both sides. Pour the cognac over them and set aflame at the table.

Serves 8–10.

Crêpes with Flaming Peach Sauce

2 3-ounce packages cream cheese, softened
4 tablespoons heavy cream
Crêpes recipe
1 package frozen sliced peaches, thawed
2 tablespoons sugar
3 tablespoons warm cognac

Beat the cream cheese and cream until light and fluffy. Spread each crêpe with some cheese and fold in quarters. Arrange in a buttered heat-proof serving dish. Place in a preheated 350° oven 10 minutes.

Meanwhile cook the peaches and sugar over low heat 5 minutes. Add the cognac, set aflame and pour over the crêpes.

Serves 4–6.

Apple Pancakes, Normandy Style

(CRÊPES NORMANDES)

¼ pound (1 stick) butter
2 cups thinly sliced apples
Crêpes recipe
⅔ cup sugar

Melt 1 tablespoon butter in a 7-inch skillet; arrange 4 slices of apples in it. Cook over low heat 2 minutes, then pour about 3 tablespoons of this batter over the apples. Sprinkle with 1 tablespoon sugar; bake 2 minutes. Turn over and bake until lightly browned. Keep warm while preparing the balance.

Makes about 12.

Crêpes with Pineapple

3 tablespoons cornstarch
⅔ cup sugar
½ teaspoon salt
2¼ cups milk, scalded
3 egg yolks
¼ pound candied pineapple, diced
¾ cup Kirsch (cherry liqueur) or Cointreau
Crêpes recipe

Mix the cornstarch, sugar and salt in the top of a double boiler. Gradually add the scalded milk, stirring constantly to prevent curdling. Cook over direct low heat, still stirring steadily, until mixture thickens. Cook 10 minutes longer.

Beat the egg yolks in a bowl; gradually add a little of the hot mixture, stirring steadily to prevent curdling. Return to top of double boiler. Place over hot water and cook 2 minutes, mixing constantly. Cool.

While the custard is cooling, marinate the pineapple in ½ cup of the liqueur. When the custard is cold, drain the pineapple and fold it in.

Put some filling on each crêpe and roll up. Arrange the crêpes on a serving dish. Pour the reserved liqueur over them and set aflame.

Serves 4–6.

Pancakes with Almond Cream

(CRÊPES AU FRANGIPANE)

Crêpes recipe
Frangipane (See p. 228)
2 squares (2 ounces) semi-sweet chocolate
2 tablespoons melted butter
1 tablespoon sugar

Spread each crêpe with 2 tablespoons of the Frangipane. Roll up and arrange in a buttered baking dish. Grate the chocolate over the crêpes, sprinkle with the butter, and then the sugar. Place in a 350° oven for 20 minutes. Serve hot.

Serves 4–6.

Belgian Pancakes with Ice Cream

(CRÊPES BRUXELLOISE)

4 tablespoons butter
½ cup sugar
¾ cup cognac or light rum, warmed
Crêpes recipe
½ pint vanilla ice cream
¼ cup slivered blanched toasted almonds

Melt the butter in a skillet; mix in the sugar until dissolved. Add the cognac or rum and set aflame. When flames die, quickly dip one crêpe at a time into the syrup. Stack on one side of the pan while dipping the remaining crêpes.

Place a crêpe on an individual plate, spread with a little ice cream and cover with another crêpe. Spoon a little syrup over it and sprinkle with the almonds. Prepare the remaining crêpes, working quickly.

Serves 6–8.

Cream Cheese Pancakes

½ pound cream cheese, softened
2 tablespoons heavy cream
3 eggs, beaten
3 tablespoons flour
2 tablespoons sugar
¼ teaspoon salt
4 tablespoons butter

Beat the cream cheese, cream and eggs together until smooth. Add the flour, sugar and salt, beating well again. Chill 30 minutes. Beat again.

Melt a little butter in a 6-inch skillet. Pour a tablespoon of the batter into it, turning the pan quickly to coat the bottom. Brown on both sides. Stack and keep warm while preparing the balance. Serve with jam or fruit sauce.

Serves 4.

Viennese Apple Pancake

(APFEL SCHMARREN)

1 cup sifted flour
1/8 teaspoon salt
2 eggs
1 cup milk
1/2 teaspoon vanilla extract
1 1/2 cups sliced apples
2 tablespoons butter
1/4 cup sugar
1 tablespoon cinnamon

Sift the flour and salt into a bowl. Beat the eggs, milk and vanilla together and add to flour, beating until smooth. Stir in the apples.

Melt the butter in a 9-inch skillet and pour the mixture into it. Bake in a 350° oven 15 minutes or until set. Tear apart with 2 forks into small pieces. Sprinkle with the sugar and cinnamon. Serves 4.

Austrian Dessert Pancakes

(PALATSCHINKEN)

1 cup raspberry or apricot jam
2 tablespoons cognac
1 cup sifted flour
1/8 teaspoon salt
5 tablespoons sugar
1 cup milk
2 eggs, beaten
4 tablespoons butter
1/4 teaspoon vanilla powder

Mix the jam with the cognac.

Sift the flour, salt and 2 tablespoons of the sugar into a bowl. Mix the milk and eggs; add to the flour mixture, stirring until very smooth.

Melt a little butter in a 9-inch skillet, tilting the pan to cover the sides. Pour in enough batter to lightly coat the bottom (about 2 tablespoons). Bake until browned on underside, then flip over with a pancake turner and brown lightly. Turn out onto a warm plate, spread lightly with jam and roll up. Put pancake into a buttered baking dish and place in a 250° oven while preparing the remaining pancakes. Arrange the pancakes in the baking dish and sprinkle the tops with the remaining sugar, mixed with the vanilla. Serve hot.

Serves 4–6.

Viennese Pancakes in Custard Sauce

(TOPFENPALATSCHINKEN)

FILLING

¼ pound (1 stick) butter
¾ cup sugar
2 egg yolks, beaten
1 teaspoon vanilla extract
1 cup cottage cheese, drained
¾ cup sour cream
½ cup seedless raisins (optional)

Cream the butter, gradually adding the sugar. Beat in the egg yolks, vanilla, cheese and sour cream. Stir in the raisins if desired.

PANCAKES

1¾ cups sifted flour
¼ teaspoon salt
1½ cups milk
3 eggs, beaten
3 tablespoons butter

Sift the flour and salt into a bowl. Beat in a mixture of the milk and eggs.

Melt a little butter in a 7-inch skillet; pour just enough batter into it to coat the bottom. Bake until lightly browned on both sides. Stack while preparing the balance. Spread some of the filling on each pancake; roll up and arrange in a buttered baking dish. Pour the Custard Sauce over them and bake in a preheated 350° oven 25 minutes or until custard is browned and set.

CUSTARD SAUCE

2 eggs
⅔ cup sugar
2½ cups milk

Beat the eggs and sugar together, then beat in the milk.
Serves 6–8.

German Pancake

(DEUTSCHE PFANNKUCHEN)

3 eggs
1 tablespoon sugar
⅛ teaspoon salt
3 tablespoons flour
⅓ cup light cream
3 tablespoons butter

Preheat oven to 425°.

Beat the eggs until light, then blend in the sugar, salt, flour and cream until very smooth. Melt the butter in an 11-inch skillet; pour the mixture into it. Bake in 425° oven 10 minutes. Reduce heat to 350° and bake 6 minutes longer or until browned and edges are puffed up. Spread with sugar, cinnamon and melted butter, or lingonberries and roll up.

Serves 2–3.

Puffed Pancake Dessert, Austrian Fashion

(GRINZINGER OMLETTEN)

4 egg yolks
3 tablespoons sugar
1 tablespoon flour
½ cup milk
1 teaspoon vanilla extract
4 egg whites
¼ teaspoon salt
2 tablespoons butter
½ cup jam
½ cup heavy cream, whipped

Beat the egg yolks in the top of a double boiler; stir in the sugar and flour. Mix in the milk. Place over hot water and cook, stirring steadily, until mixture coats the spoon. Remove from the heat and stir in the vanilla. Cool.

Beat the egg whites and salt until stiff. Gradually fold them into the yolk mixture. Melt the butter in 2 9-inch baking pans; divide the mixture between them. Bake in a preheated 350° oven 20 minutes or until light brown and puffed. Cover with the jam and whipped cream and serve at once.

Serves 4–6.

Emperor's Omelet Pancake

(KAISERSCHMARREN)

½ cup seedless raisins
¼ cup cognac
5 egg yolks
½ cup sugar
2 cups sifted flour
1 cup heavy cream
5 egg whites
⅛ teaspoon salt
4 tablespoons butter
Confectioners' sugar

Preheat oven to 350°.

Soak the raisins in the cognac.

Beat the egg yolks until thick and light. Beat in ¼ cup of the sugar. Add the flour, alternately with the cream, mixing until smooth. Beat the egg whites and salt until stiff; fold into the previous mixture. Turn into a buttered 2-quart baking dish. Bake 30 minutes or until browned and set.

The next part of the preparation is unusual. Tear the baked pancake into pieces with 2 forks. Melt the butter in a skillet; add the torn pancakes, the drained raisins and the remaining sugar. Cook over low heat, stirring constantly, until pieces are coated with the sugar. Sprinkle with confectioners' sugar and serve hot.

Serves 4–6.

Hungarian Berry Pancakes

PANCAKES

2 cups sifted flour
¼ teaspoon salt
½ teaspoon powdered ginger
1 egg
2 cups sour cream
Butter

Sift the flour, salt and ginger into a bowl. Beat the egg, then mix in the sour cream. Add to the flour mixture, stirring until smooth. The batter should be fairly thin, like heavy cream, so add a little more cream if necessary.

Melt a little butter in a 6-inch skillet. Pour about 1 tablespoon of the batter into it and tilt the pan to make a thin coat on the bottom. Bake until lightly browned on both sides. Stack while preparing the balance of the pancakes.

BERRIES

2 cups raspberries or sliced strawberries
½ cup sugar
½ cup slivered blanched almonds

Toss the berries lightly with the sugar. Place a heaping tablespoon of the berries on each pancake and roll up. Arrange in a single layer in a shallow buttered baking dish and sprinkle with the almonds. Place in a preheated 475° oven 5 minutes.

Makes about 24.

Swedish Dessert Pancakes

(PLÄTTAR)

1 cup sifted flour
1 tablespoon sugar
⅛ teaspoon salt
3 eggs, beaten
2 cups milk
Butter
Confectioners' sugar
Lingonberries or canned whole cranberries

Sift the flour, sugar and salt into a bowl. Beat in the eggs and milk until very smooth. Chill 2 hours.

Special *plättar* pans are available. They are large skillets with small (about 2½ inches) round depressions. Melt a little butter in each depression and pour just enough batter into them to cover the bottoms thinly. Bake until browned on both sides. Stack and keep warm while preparing the balance of the batter. If you don't have a *plättar* pan, use a heavy skillet and make small pancakes. Sprinkle the pancakes with confectioners' sugar and serve with the lingonberries or cranberries.

Makes about 36.

Dessert Omelet

(OMELETTE AU CONFITURE)

4 egg yolks
¼ teaspoon salt
4 egg whites, stiffly beaten
2 tablespoons butter
4 tablespoons raspberry or strawberry preserves
2 tablespoons confectioners' sugar
3 tablespoons warm cognac

Preheat oven to 400°.

Beat the egg yolks and salt until light. Fold in the egg whites. Melt the butter in a 9- or 10-inch skillet; pour in the egg mixture. Cook over low heat until bottom is delicately browned, then bake 5 minutes or until set and top browned. Spread with the preserves. Roll up and turn out onto a heated serving dish. Sprinkle with the sugar. Place under the broiler until sugar browns lightly.

Pour the cognac over the omelet and set aflame.

Serves 3–4.

Meringue Pancakes

(SALZBURGER NOCKERLN)

4 egg yolks
¼ cup sifted flour
⅛ teaspoon salt
8 egg whites
¾ cup sugar
½ teaspoon vanilla extract
4 tablespoons butter

Preheat oven to 275°.

Beat the egg yolks until thick and light. Mix in the flour and salt until well blended.

Beat the egg whites until peaks form. Very gradually beat in the sugar until very stiff. Fold into the yolk mixture with the vanilla.

Melt the butter in a 9-inch skillet, tilting the pan to coat the sides. Drop the meringue into it in 8 mounds. Cook over low heat 3 minutes, or until underside is lightly browned, then bake 10 minutes or until top is delicately browned. Serve at once, sprinkled with sugar if desired.

Serves 8.

Baked Dessert Pancake

2 tablespoons butter
3 eggs
½ teaspoon salt
⅓ cup sifted flour
2 tablespoons sugar
½ cup milk

Preheat oven to 450°.

Place the butter in a 10-inch skillet (with ovenproof handle) and set in the oven to melt while preparing the batter. The butter must be hot and well distributed before the batter is poured into it.

Beat the eggs and salt until light. Sift in the flour and sugar, beating until well blended. Beat in the milk. Pour the batter into the skillet. Bake 15 minutes or until puffy and brown. (The surface will be irregular.) Spread with selected filling and roll up. Turn out into a heated serving dish.

Serves 2.

SUGGESTED FILLINGS

Sugar and cinnamon, lingonberries, apple sauce, honey or jam.

Italian Pear Meringue Pancakes

PEAR FILLING

1 pound pears, peeled, cored and cubed
½ cup sugar

Cook the pears and sugar over low heat until very thick and dry. Cool.

PANCAKES

3 egg yolks
¾ cup milk
¾ cup water
1 tablespoon sugar
3 tablespoons cognac
1½ cups sifted flour
¼ teaspoon salt
¼ cup melted butter
2 tablespoons vegetable oil
2 tablespoons butter

Beat the egg yolks. Mix in the milk and water, then the sugar, cognac, flour and salt until very smooth. Stir in the butter. (If you have an electric blender, combine all the ingredients and blend until smooth.) Chill 2 hours.

Heat a little oil and butter in a 6-inch skillet; pour in enough batter to just coat the pan. Cook until delicately browned on both sides. Stack while preparing the balance. Place a tablespoon of the pear mixture on each pancake and roll up. Arrange in a buttered baking dish.

MERINGUE

2 egg whites | *¼ cup sugar*

Preheat oven to 450°.

Beat the egg whites until soft peaks form, then very gradually beat in the sugar until very stiff. Heap over the pancakes. Bake 5 minutes or until delicately browned.

Makes 12 pancakes.

Soufflés and Other Specialties

Vanilla Soufflé

(SOUFFLÉ À LA VANILLE)

4 tablespoons sifted flour
1 cup milk
½ cup plus 1 tablespoon sugar
5 egg yolks
2 tablespoons vanilla extract
2 tablespoons softened butter
6 egg whites
⅛ teaspoon salt

Preheat oven to 375°.

Butter a 2-quart soufflé dish and dust with sugar.

In a saucepan mix the flour with a little milk until smooth, then add the rest of the milk and ½ cup of the sugar. Cook over medium heat, stirring constantly just to the boiling point, then cook over low heat 3 minutes.

Beat the egg yolks in a bowl; gradually add the hot mixture, stirring steadily to prevent curdling. Blend in the vanilla and butter. Cool.

Beat the egg whites and salt until soft peaks form, then beat in the remaining tablespoon of sugar until mixture is stiff but not dry. Stir one-fourth of the egg whites into the previous mixture; then carefully fold in the remaining egg whites. Turn into the prepared soufflé dish. Bake 35 minutes or until puffed and browned. Serve at once.

Serves 4–6.

VARIATIONS

Coffee Soufflé (SOUFFLÉ AU CAFÉ).

Dissolve 4 teaspoons instant coffee in the milk; proceed as directed.

Orange Soufflé (SOUFFLE À L'ORANGE).

Add 3 tablespoons grated orange rind and ⅓ cup orange liqueur to the yolk mixture. Reduce vanilla to 1 teaspoon. Proceed as directed.

Candied Fruit Soufflé (SOUFFLÉ ROTHSCHILD).

Marinate ¾ cup diced candied fruits in ⅓ cup Kirsch or Grand Marnier 30 minutes. Drain and add to the yolk mixture. Reduce vanilla to 2 teaspoons. Proceed as directed.

Almond Soufflé (SOUFFLÉ AUX AMANDES).

Add ½ cup finely ground toasted almonds and ½ teaspoon almond extract to the yolk mixture. Proceed as directed.

Chocolate Soufflé

(SOUFFLÉ AU CHOCOLAT)

3 ounces (3 squares) semi-sweet chocolate
2 tablespoons brewed coffee
3 tablespoons butter
3 tablespoons flour
1 cup milk
½ cup sugar
4 egg yolks
5 egg whites
⅛ teaspoon salt

Butter a 2-quart soufflé dish and dust with sugar.

Melt the chocolate in the coffee over hot water.

Melt the butter in a saucepan. Remove from the heat and blend in the flour. Gradually add the milk, then stir in ⅓ cup of the sugar. Return to the heat and cook, stirring constantly to the boiling point; then cook over low heat 5 minutes. Beat the egg yolks in a bowl; gradually add the hot mixture, stirring steadily to prevent curdling. Blend in the chocolate. Cool.

Beat the egg whites and salt until soft peaks form, then

gradually beat in the remaining sugar until the whites are stiff but not dry. Fold into the chocolate mixture. Turn into the soufflé dish. Bake in a preheated 375° oven 35 minutes or until puffed and fairly firm when dish is shaken. Serve at once.

Serves 6–8.

French Cold Chocolate Soufflé

(SOUFFLÉ GLACÉ)

3 ounces sweet chocolate
6 tablespoons water
2 teaspoons instant coffee
1 envelope (1 tablespoon) gelatin
3 egg yolks
3 whole eggs
¼ cup sugar
1 cup heavy cream

Melt the chocolate in 2 tablespoons of the water over low heat. Stir in the coffee. Cool. Soften the gelatin in the remaining water, then place over hot water, stirring until dissolved.

In the top of a double boiler, beat the egg yolks and whole eggs; gradually beat in the sugar until light. Place over hot water and cook, stirring constantly until thickened. Stir in the chocolate and gelatin. Cool 20 minutes, then beat with an electric mixer or rotary beater 5 minutes.

Whip the cream and fold into the chocolate mixture. Turn into a 1½-quart soufflé dish. Chill until set. Serve with whipped cream or Chocolate Sauce.

Serves 6–8.

Frozen Peach Soufflé

(SOUFFLÉ GLACÉ AUX PÊCHES)

1½ pounds fresh peaches
1 cup fine sugar
2 egg whites
1 tablespoon lemon juice
2 tablespoons orange liqueur
1 cup heavy cream, whipped

Peel the peaches and cut them into small pieces; place in the dry large bowl of an electric mixer (not an electric blender). Turn mixer on low speed, and beat until pulpy. Add the sugar and egg whites, and beat at medium speed until the mixture forms into very stiff peaks (about 10 minutes).

While mixture is beating, put a doubled waxed paper collar around a 1-quart soufflé dish, to come 2 inches above the top edge of the dish. Fasten with scotch tape to hold in place.

Stir the lemon juice and liqueur into the peach mixture, then fold in the whipped cream. Turn into the soufflé dish slowly. Cover the top with aluminum foil or waxed paper, and freeze overnight. Remove from freezer about 15 minutes before serving. Accompany or decorate with sliced peaches, which have been previously marinated in orange liqueur, if desired.

Serves 8.

French Provincial Chocolate Fondue

(FONDUE AU CHOCOLAT)

2 squares (2 ounces) unsweetened chocolate
1 cup light cream
½ cup sugar
¼ teaspoon salt
1 tablespoon butter
3 egg yolks
1 cup fresh bread crumbs
3 egg whites, beaten stiff

Break the chocolate into small pieces and combine in a saucepan with the cream. Place over low heat until chocolate melts, stirring frequently. Stir in the sugar, salt and butter until dissolved.

Beat the egg yolks in a bowl; gradually add the hot mixture, stirring steadily to prevent curdling. Mix in the crumbs and let cool. Fold in the egg whites. Turn into a 1½-quart buttered baking dish. Bake in a preheated 350° oven 40 minutes. Serve hot with whipped cream or Foamy Sauce.

Serves 4–6.

Chocolate Dessert, Parisian Style

(SUPRÊME AU CHOCOLAT)

2 *squares (2 ounces) unsweetened chocolate*
2 *ounces sweet chocolate*
¼ *cup sugar*
4 *egg yolks*
2 *tablespoons cognac*
7 *tablespoons softened butter*
4 *egg whites*

Rub a 1-quart mold or dish with vegetable oil.

Break the chocolate into small pieces and let melt over hot water. Remove from the heat and mix in the sugar. Add 1 egg yolk at a time, beating after each addition. Then mix in the cognac and butter. Beat until very smooth.

Beat the egg whites until stiff but not dry and fold into the chocolate mixture. Pour into the prepared mold. Chill, overnight if possible. Carefully turn out and serve with Vanilla Sauce or whipped cream.

Serves 4–6.

Chocolate Charlotte, Basque Fashion

(CHARLOTTE BASQUE)

3 squares (3 ounces) semi-sweet chocolate
1¾ cups milk
4 egg yolks
½ cup sugar
1 teaspoon vanilla extract
16 ladyfingers, split
½ pound (2 sticks) sweet butter
1¼ cups finely ground almonds
2 tablespoons cognac

Break the chocolate into small pieces and combine with the milk in a saucepan. Cook over low heat, stirring constantly, until chocolate melts.

Beat the egg yolks in a saucepan; gradually add the sugar, then the melted chocolate, beating constantly to prevent curdling. Cook over low heat, stirring steadily, until mixture coats the spoon, but do not let boil. Add vanilla. Cool.

Line the bottom of a buttered 7-inch mold with waxed paper. Then line the bottom and sides with ladyfingers (about 16 of the halves).

Cream the butter, then mix in the almonds. Add the cooled chocolate mixture and the cognac, beating until smooth. Make layers of this mixture and the remaining ladyfingers in the lined mold. Top layer should be the chocolate mixture. Chill overnight. Carefully unmold and serve with whipped cream if desired.

Serves 8–10.

French Strawberry Charlotte

(CHARLOTTE MALAKOFF AUX FRAISES)

1 quart strawberries
1 cup orange or cherry liqueur
½ cup water
16 ladyfingers, split
½ pound (2 sticks) sweet butter
1 cup superfine sugar
¼ teaspoon almond extract
1¼ cups finely ground almonds
2 cups heavy cream, whipped

Hull the strawberries, wash and dry.

Put ½ cup of the liqueur and the water into a deep dish. Dip the ladyfingers in the mixture and drain on a rack. Line the bottom of a buttered 7-inch mold with a piece of waxed paper, then line the bottom and sides with about half of the split ladyfingers.

Cream the butter and sugar until light and fluffy. Beat in the almond extract and remaining liqueur until sugar is dissolved. Stir in the almonds, then fold in the cream.

Spread one-third of the mixture in the lined mold. Cover with half the strawberries, then add a layer of ladyfingers. Repeat the layers of cream, berries and ladyfingers, then a layer of cream and ladyfingers. Cover the top with a piece of waxed paper, and weight it down with a saucer. Chill overnight, then carefully unmold. Serve with additional whipped cream if desired.

Serves 8–10.

Dessert Cheese Mold, Parisian Fashion

(COEUR À LA CRÈME)

1 *pound cream cheese*
1 *pound cottage cheese, drained*
⅛ *teaspoon salt*
2 *cups heavy cream*

Traditionally *coeur à la crème* is heart-shaped. If you haven't a heart-shaped basket, use a round or oblong straw basket. A basket is necessary to allow the cheese to drain. Line it with wet cheesecloth.

Beat together the cream cheese, cottage cheese and salt until thoroughly smooth. Gradually stir in the cream. Turn into the basket and place a bowl underneath to catch the liquid. Refrigerate overnight.

Unmold onto a serving dish just before serving. Surround with strawberries or raspberries and serve with a bowl of powdered sugar, strawberry jam or Bar-le-Duc (French preserve).

Serves 6–8.

Russian Easter Dessert

(PASHKA)

2 pounds cottage cheese
¼ pound (1 stick) butter, softened
½ cup sour cream
1 egg
¾ cup sugar
1 cup ground almonds

Force the cheese through a sieve. Cream the butter and sour cream together until smooth. Add the cheese, egg, sugar and almonds. Mix well.

Line a *pashka* basket or colander with a napkin. Pour cheese mixture into it. Cover with a napkin and then a heavy plate, pressing down well. Chill 24 hours, with a bowl underneath to catch the draining liquid. Carefully turn the Pashka onto a serving dish.

Serves 8–10.

Note: A half cup chopped candied fruits may be added to the mixture, if you like.

Italian Chocolate-Almond Clusters

(CROCANTINI DI MANDORLE)

½ pound (8 squares) unsweetened chocolate
¼ cup sugar
1½ cups split blanched toasted almonds

Break the chocolate into small pieces and combine with the sugar in the top of a double boiler. Place over hot water and cook, stirring frequently, until chocolate is melted and smooth. Mix in the almonds until well blended. Drop the mixture by the teaspoon onto a greased baking sheet, leaving about 1 inch between each mound. Keep in a cool place (not the refrigerator) until firm. To store, place in an airtight container in layers, with aluminum foil or waxed paper between.

Makes about 1 pound.

Italian Rice-Nut Dessert

(RISO E MANDORLE)

1½ cups raw long grain rice
4 cups milk
1 teaspoon salt
½ cup Marsala or sweet sherry
¾ cup sugar
¾ cup ground almonds
3 egg yolks, beaten

Wash the rice under cold running water. Drain. Combine with the milk and salt; let stand 1 hour. Add the wine. Bring to a boil, then cook over low heat 15 minutes. Cool 10 minutes; mix in the sugar, almonds and egg yolks. Turn into a buttered baking dish. Bake in a preheated 350° oven 20 minutes. Chill.

Serves 4–6.

Parisian Rice and Fruit Mold

(RIZ A L'IMPERATRICE)

4¼ cups water
1 cup long grain rice
½ teaspoon salt
3 cups milk
1 envelope (1 tablespoon) gelatin
4 egg yolks
⅔ cup sugar
1 cup finely chopped candied fruits
2 tablespoons fruit liqueur
1 cup heavy cream, whipped

Bring 4 cups of the water to a boil; add the rice. Cook over high heat 4 minutes, then drain. Put the rice in a saucepan and add the salt and 1½ cups of the milk. Cover and cook over very low heat 25 minutes or until the rice is tender.

While the rice is cooking, soften the gelatin in the remaining water. Beat the egg yolks in the top of a double boiler. Mix in the sugar, then the remaining milk. Place over hot water and cook, stirring constantly, until mixture thickens and coats the spoon. Stir in the gelatin until dissolved.

Mix custard with the rice, and chill until mixture begins to set. Mix the fruits with the liqueur and let stand 5 minutes. Fold into the rice mixture with the whipped cream. Turn into a 2-quart mold and chill until set.

Carefully unmold; decorate with whipped cream and candied cherries if desired.

Serves 8–10.

Chilled Apricot Mold

24 ladyfingers
¼ pound (1 stick) butter
1¾ cups superfine sugar
4 egg yolks
3 jars strained apricots (baby food)
2 cups vanilla wafer crumbs
1 envelope (1 tablespoon) gelatin
¼ cup cognac or fruit liqueur
2 cups heavy cream, whipped stiff

Split the ladyfingers and line a buttered 10-inch spring form pan with them.

Cream the butter and sugar until light and fluffy. Beat in the egg yolks. Mix in the apricots and crumbs. Turn into a saucepan and cook, stirring constantly, until thickened and smooth.

Soften the gelatin in the liqueur, then place over hot water and stir until dissolved. Stir into the apricot mixture and cool. Fold in the whipped cream and turn into the lined pan. Chill overnight. Remove the rim of the pan, and decorate the top with additional whipped cream and nuts or candied fruit if desired.

Serves 10–12.

Persian Halva

½ cup vegetable oil
1 cup rice flour or cornstarch
4 cups milk
¼ cup rose water
½ cup granulated sugar
1 teaspoon ground cardamom
½ cup sifted confectioners' sugar
½ cup chopped pistachio nuts or blanched almonds

Heat the oil in a saucepan; stir in the flour until lightly browned. Gradually add the milk, stirring until smooth over low heat. Add the rose water, granulated sugar and cardamom. Cook, stirring constantly, until thickened. Mix in the confectioners' sugar, stirring until dissolved.

Rinse a shallow pan with cold water, and pour the mixture into it to a depth of 1 inch; sprinkle with the nuts and cool until firm. Cut into oblong pieces.

Serves 8–10.

Note: Rose water is obtainable in specialty food shops or drug stores.

Indian Carrot Dessert

(INDIAN HALVA)

2 pounds carrots
1 cup sugar
¼ cup water
Pinch saffron
4 tablespoons butter
3 cups finely ground blanched almonds
¼ teaspoon nutmeg

Pare the carrots, cut into small pieces and run in an electric blender a little at a time until very fine. (Or grate fine.) Barely cover the carrots with water, bring to a boil and cook 15 minutes or until carrots are very soft. Drain if any liquid remains.

Cook the sugar and water until a thread forms when a fork is dipped in and raised. Add the carrots and saffron; cook over low heat, stirring steadily, until carrots absorb the sugar syrup. Mix in the butter, then the almonds. Spoon into 6 to 8 glasses, sprinkle with nutmeg and serve at room temperature.

Greek Halva

1 cup sugar
1 cup honey
2 cups water
½ teaspoon cinnamon
¼ pound (1 stick) butter
½ cup ground almonds
1 cup Cream of Wheat

Combine the sugar, honey, water and cinnamon in a saucepan. Bring to a boil and cook over low heat 20 minutes. While the syrup is cooking, melt the butter in a skillet; add the almonds and Cream of Wheat. Cook over low heat, stirring steadily until browned.

After syrup has cooked 20 minutes add browned almonds and Cream of Wheat. Mix well, cover and cook 15 minutes, stirring occasionally. Pour into a buttered 8- by 10-inch shallow pan. Cool. Cut into squares and sprinkle with confectioners' sugar or additional cinnamon.

Makes 20 2-inch squares.

Indian Vermicelli Dessert

(SEVIAN)

3 tablespoons honey
3 tablespoons sugar
1 cup water
1¾ cups vermicelli (very thin noodles)
6 tablespoons butter
¼ cup slivered blanched almonds
¼ teaspoon nutmeg

Combine the honey, sugar and water in a saucepan; bring to a boil and cook over high heat 4 minutes. While the syrup is cooking, break the vermicelli into small pieces. Melt the butter in a skillet; add the vermicelli and cook, stirring continuously until browned. Add the almonds, then the syrup, mixing well. Cook until syrup is absorbed. Mix in the nutmeg. Serve hot.

Serves 4–6.

Siamese Tapioca Dessert

1 cup water
¼ teaspoon salt
⅓ cup quick-cooking tapioca
½ cup sugar
2 egg yolks
1½ cups orange juice
1 tablespoon lemon juice
2 egg whites
1 cup finely diced fresh fruits (grapes, bananas, oranges)

In a saucepan, combine the water, salt, tapioca and ¼ cup of the sugar. Cook over low heat, stirring constantly, until tapioca is translucent (about 5 minutes).

Beat the egg yolks until thick, then mix in the orange and lemon juice. Gradually add the hot tapioca mixture, stirring steadily to prevent curdling. Return to saucepan and cook, stirring constantly for 3 minutes, but do not let boil. Cool 15 minutes.

Beat the egg whites until soft peaks form, then gradually beat in the remaining sugar until stiff. Fold into the tapioca mixture, then fold in the fruits. Spoon into parfait glasses or sherbet cups and chill.

Serves 6.

Spanish Bread Dessert

White bread
2 egg yolks
⅛ teaspoon salt
½ cup sweet sherry
½ cup vegetable oil
Powdered sugar
Fruit jam

Buy an unsliced loaf of bread and from it cut 6 slices ½-inch thick. Trim off the crusts and cut slices into triangles.

Beat the egg yolks, salt and sherry in a broad, deep dish. Place the bread in it until well soaked.

Heat the oil in a skillet; brown the bread in it on both sides. Drain, sprinkle with sugar and spread a little jam on each piece.

Serves 6.

Fruits

Cherries Imperial

(CERISES À LA RUSSE)

2 cups fresh or canned pitted sweet cherries
⅓ cup sugar
½ cup cognac
1½ envelopes (1½ tablespoons) gelatin
1½ cups dry white wine
1 tablespoon lemon juice
Blanched toasted almonds

Sprinkle the cherries with the sugar. (Use only ¼ cup for canned cherries). Cover and chill 1 hour. Drain the juice into a measuring cup. Add the cognac and enough water to make 1 cup.

Soften the gelatin in ½ cup of the wine. Place over hot water and stir until dissolved. Mix in the remaining wine, the cherry liquid and the lemon juice. Using half the mixture, spoon into 8 custard cups until half full. Chill until set. Put an almond in each cherry and arrange over the set gelatin. Cover with the remaining gelatin mixture. Chill until firm. Unmold and serve with whipped cream.

Serves 8.

Cherries in Cognac Custard

(CERISES AU COGNAC)

1 No. 2½ can pitted Bing cherries
5 egg yolks
2 tablespoons heavy cream
½ cup sugar
⅛ teaspoon salt
3 tablespoons cognac
⅛ teaspoon almond extract

Drain the cherries, reserving 1 cup juice. Chill the cherries.

Beat the egg yolks, cream, sugar and salt in a saucepan. Mix in the cognac and reserved cherry juice. Cook over low heat, stirring constantly until thickened, but do not let boil. Stir in the almond extract. Cool, stirring occasionally. Pour over the cherries and chill.

Serves 4–6.

Strawberry Meringue

1 quart strawberries
¼ cup fruit liqueur
2 egg whites
¼ cup confectioners' sugar

Preheat oven to 425°.

Wash, hull and dry the berries. Arrange them in a buttered shallow baking dish; sprinkle with the liqueur.

Beat the egg whites until peaks form, then gradually beat in the confectioners' sugar until whites are stiff. Put through a pastry tube and make a decorative border around the dish, or pile over the berries with a spoon. Bake 5 minutes or until delicately browned. Serve at once.

Serves 4–6.

Strawberries with Meringue, Italian Style

(FRAGOLE DAMA BIANCA)

1 quart strawberries
½ cup sugar
¼ cup Grand Marnier or Curaçao
2 egg whites
¾ cup heavy cream

Hull, wash and dry the berries. Sprinkle with 2 tablespoons of the sugar and the liqueur. Chill several hours.

One hour before serving, beat the egg whites until soft peaks form, then gradually beat in the remaining sugar until stiff. Whip the cream and fold into the meringue. Pour over the berries and chill. (The meringue will collapse if prepared too soon.)

Serves 6–8.

Strawberries Romanoff

1 pint strawberries, washed, hulled and drained
¼ cup powdered sugar
1 pint vanilla ice cream
1 cup heavy cream, whipped
2 tablespoons cognac

Sprinkle the berries with the sugar and chill until ready to use.

Beat the ice cream until fluffy; fold in the whipped cream and cognac. Pour over the berries and mix lightly.

Serves 8–10.

Pears Helene, French Style

(POIRES HÉLÈNE)

3 large firm pears
⅔ cup sugar
1¾ cups water
1 teaspoon vanilla extract
1 pint vanilla ice cream
Chocolate Sauce

Peel the pears, cut in half lengthwise and core. Bring the sugar and water to a boil, cook 5 minutes then add the pears. Cover and cook until tender but still firm, turning the pears once or twice. Mix in the vanilla extract and let pears cool in the syrup. Drain. Place each pear half in a deep dish. Fill the scooped out put with ice cream. Serve with a bowl of hot Chocolate Sauce.

Serves 6.

Baked Pears in Red Wine

(POIRES AU VIN ROUGE)

8 firm pears
1⅛ cups sugar
1 teaspoon vanilla extract
4 cups dry red wine

Preheat oven to 350°.

Peel the pears, but leave stems on. In a baking dish, mix together the sugar, vanilla and wine. Arrange the pears in it. Cover the dish and bake 50 minutes or until pears are tender but firm. Baste and turn pears frequently. Chill.

Serves 8.

Baked Pears in Cream

(POIRES SAVOIE)

6 firm pears
¾ cup powdered sugar
3 tablespoons butter
½ cup hot heavy cream

Preheat oven to 400°.

Peel and quarter the pears. Arrange in a baking dish, sprinkle with the sugar and dot with the butter. Bake 30 minutes or until pears are tender and sugar dark brown. Baste frequently. Add the cream. (Be sure it's hot, particularly if you're using a glass dish.) Bake 10 minutes longer. Serve hot.

Serves 6–8.

Baked Apples in Wine

(APFEL IN WEIN)

6 large tart firm apples
6 tablespoons currant jelly
1 cup dry white wine
¼ cup sugar

Preheat oven to 375°.

Peel and core the apples. Place a tablespoon of jelly in each. Arrange the apples in a baking dish. Add the wine mixed with the sugar. Bake 35 minutes or until the apples are tender, basting frequently. Serve hot or cold.

Serves 6.

Sautéed Apple Dessert

(POUDING ALSACIEN)

2½ pounds firm tart apples
¼ pound (1 stick) butter
¾ cup apricot jam, sieved
2 tablespoons cognac
½ cup granulated sugar
3 egg yolks
1 tablespoon flour
1 cup fresh fine bread crumbs
½ teaspoon cinnamon
2 egg whites
⅛ teaspoon salt
Confectioners' sugar

Peel and core the apples, quarter and cut in ¼-inch slices. Melt 4 tablespoons of the butter in a skillet; sauté the apples 1 layer at a time until delicately browned. As apples are browned, place in a 9-inch buttered baking dish. When all are browned, lightly mix in the jam mixed with the cognac. Smooth the top.

Cream until light and fluffy the remaining butter and all but 2 teaspoons of the sugar. Beat in the egg yolks, then the flour, bread crumbs and cinnamon. Beat the egg whites and salt until soft peaks form, then beat in the remaining 2 teaspoons of sugar until mixture is stiff. Fold into the yolk mixture. Spread over the apples. Bake in a preheated 325° oven 25 minutes. Sprinkle with confectioners' sugar and bake 10 minutes longer. Cool, then chill overnight.

Serves 6–8.

English Apple Hedgehog

3 pounds apples
¾ cup sugar
¼ cup water
2 tablespoons lemon juice
1 envelope (1 tablespoon) gelatin
3 tablespoons sweet sherry
3 drops red food coloring
½ cup sliced blanched almonds

Peel, core and cut the apples into small pieces. Combine with the sugar, water and lemon juice in a saucepan. Cook over low heat until tender, about 20 minutes. Shake the pan every few minutes to prevent scorching.

While the apples are cooking, soften the gelatin in the sherry. Stir into the hot cooked apples until dissolved. Purée mixture in an electric blender or force through a sieve. Taste for sweetness and mix in the food coloring.

Rinse a round or melon mold with cold water and turn the apple mixture into it. Chill until firm, unmold and stud all over with the almonds.

Serves 6–8.

Australian Caramel Apples

6 baking apples
1⅓ cups firmly packed brown sugar
6 tablespoons butter
½ cup water
¼ cup cognac

Preheat oven to 350°.

Wash and core the apples. Place a tablespoon of the brown sugar in each, then a tablespoon of butter. Arrange in a buttered baking dish.

Cook the water, cognac and remaining brown sugar 10 minutes or until syrupy. Pour over the apples. Bake 35 minutes or until tender, basting frequently. Chill. Serve with whipped cream or Foamy Sauce if desired.

Serves 6.

Portuguese Poached Apples with Meringue

6 baking apples
½ cup port wine
¾ cup orange juice
¾ cup sugar
6 maraschino cherries
3 egg whites
½ pint firm vanilla ice cream

Wash and core the apples; peel half way down. Arrange them in a deep skillet. Add a mixture of the port, orange juice and ½ cup of the sugar. Bring to a boil, cover and cook over low heat 35 minutes or until tender. Baste occasionally. Cool in the syrup, basting frequently. Drain and place a cherry in each apple. Arrange in a heatproof serving dish.

Beat the egg whites until soft peaks form. Gradually beat in the remaining sugar until mixture is stiff but not dry. Put some ice cream in each apple, then cover completely with the meringue. Bake in a preheated 425° oven 5 minutes or until meringue is delicately browned. Serve at once, or place in the freezer until ice cold.

Serves 6.

Hungarian Plum Dumplings

(SZILVAS GOMBOC)

12 small black (Italian) plums
12 cubes sugar
2 cups sifted flour
1 teaspoon salt
6 tablespoons butter
2 cups cold mashed potatoes
2 eggs
¾ cup dry bread crumbs

Wash and dry the plums; carefully remove the pits and replace each with a cube of sugar.

Sift the flour and salt into a bowl; cut in 3 tablespoons of the butter. Knead in the potatoes, then the eggs, until very smooth. Roll out the dough ¼-inch thick on a well-floured surface. Cut into 3-inch squares. Put a plum in the center of each and bring up the ends; moisten edges with a little water and seal. With floured hands, press the dough around the plums.

Use a large kettle of boiling water and cook the dumplings in it 15 minutes. Don't crowd the dumplings in the pan. Drain well.

Melt the remaining butter and toss with the bread crumbs. Sprinkle over the dumplings.

Serves 4–6.

Note: Small apricots or cherries may be prepared in the same manner.

Chinese Sesame Seed Bananas

2 cups sugar
¾ cup water
½ cup sesame seeds
4 firm bananas
¼ cup sifted cornstarch
3 tablespoons butter

Cook the sugar and water until syrupy and thick. Mix in the sesame seeds.

While the syrup is cooking, peel the bananas and cut into 2-inch lengths. Roll them in the cornstarch. Melt the butter in a skillet. Lightly brown the bananas in it.

The method of serving is unusual. Put some ice water in a serving bowl. Using a fork, dip the banana pieces in the hot syrup, coating them thoroughly. Each person served then dips the banana in the ice water, which will produce a thin glaze on the bananas.

Serves 4.

Note: Peeled apple wedges may be prepared in the same manner.

Rhubarb Fool

2 pounds rhubarb
¾ cup sugar
¾ cup heavy cream

Wash the rhubarb and cut into small pieces. Combine with the sugar in a skillet. Cook over low heat, stirring frequently, 15 minutes, or until rhubarb is very tender and dry. Taste for sweetness. Purée in an electric blender or force through a sieve. Cool. Mix in the cream and chill.

Serves 4–6.

Cranberry Fool

1 3-ounce package cream cheese, softened
⅛ teaspoon salt
¼ cup light corn syrup
1 1-pound can whole cranberry sauce
1 cup heavy cream, whipped

Beat the cheese, salt and corn syrup until smooth. Mix in the cranberries, then fold in the whipped cream. Spoon into sherbet dishes and freeze until firm.

Serves 4–6.

English Gooseberry Fool

2 pounds gooseberries
¼ cup water
1 cup sugar
1 tablespoon butter
1 cup heavy cream, whipped

Preheat oven to 300°.

Wash the gooseberries, discarding the stems. Combine with the water in a baking dish. Cover and bake until very soft, about

20 minutes. Stir occasionally. Mix in the sugar and butter; taste for sweetness. Purée in an electric blender or force through a sieve. Chill, then fold in the whipped cream. Serve in glass dishes.

Serves 4–6.

Note: Any berry may be prepared in the same manner.

Macedoine of Fruits

Any combination of fresh raw fruits may be used. Cubed pineapple, peeled sliced peaches, diced oranges, grapes and strawberries is just one combination. Marinate the fruits in a fruit liqueur, cognac or port wine in the refrigerator several hours. Serve very cold.

Persian Melon Delight

1 *Persian melon or large cantaloupe*
2 *peaches, peeled and sliced thin*
2 *tablespoons lemon juice*
⅓ *cup sugar*
¼ *teaspoon salt*
2 *tablespoons rose water or cognac*
Finely crushed ice

Cut the melon in half, discard the seeds and make as many melon balls as possible. Put all the juice and the melon balls in a bowl. Add the peaches, lemon juice, sugar, salt and rose water or cognac. Mix well and chill.

Just before serving, divide the fruit among 6 dishes, and put some crushed ice in the center.

Serves 6.

Note: Rose water is obtainable in specialty food shops or drug stores. Cognac is not an authentic substitute, but it may be used.

Oranges in Syrup

(ORANGES GLACÉES)

6 large oranges
3 tablespoons orange liqueur
⅔ cup water
2 cups granulated sugar

Buy navel oranges if possible. Wash and dry. Carefully peel the skins. (A vegetable peeler is good for this purpose.) Cut the peel into narrow strips. Cover the peel with water, bring to a boil and cook over low heat 10 minutes. Drain and dry. Add the liqueur and let stand while preparing the oranges.

Remove all the white part of the oranges. If they won't stand upright, cut a slice off one end. Arrange in a serving dish.

Boil the water and sugar until a little dropped into a glass of cold water forms a firm ball. Spoon over the oranges slowly, using up all the syrup. Chill. Drain the orange peel and spoon around the oranges.

Serves 6.

Apricot Compote

(MARILLENKOMPOTT)

1 pound dried apricots
2 cups cider
2 tablespoons sugar
2 tablespoons butter
¼ cup slivered blanched almonds

Wash the apricots, cover with boiling water and drain immediately. In a saucepan, combine the apricots and cider. Let soak 3 hours. Add the sugar, bring to a boil and cook over low heat 30 minutes or until tender. Mix in the butter. Chill and serve sprinkled with the almonds.

Serves 4–6.

Prune Compote

1 pound prunes
1 cup orange juice
2 cups water
⅓ cup sugar
1 lemon, thinly sliced
½ cup blanched almonds

Wash the prunes. Soak in the orange juice mixed with the water 1 hour, then bring to a boil. Add the sugar and lemon. Cook over low heat 15 minutes or until almost tender. Add the whole almonds; cook 5 minutes longer. Cool.

Serves 4–6.

Peach Compote with Jelly

2 pounds peaches
1½ cups water
½ cup dry white wine
¾ cup sugar
1 tablespoon lemon juice
2 teaspoons grated lemon rind
Currant jelly

Wash the peaches, plunge into boiling water, then peel, cut in half and discard the pits.

Bring the water, wine and sugar to a boil. Add the peaches, lemon juice and rind. Cover and cook over low heat 10 minutes or until tender but firm. Remove the peaches and arrange in a serving dish, cut side up. Boil the liquid until syrupy. Cool. Place a teaspoon of jelly in each peach half and pour the syrup over them. Chill.

Serves 6–8.

German Prune Whip

(PFLAUMEN MIT PORTWEIN)

1 pound prunes
¾ cup sugar
1 tablespoon cornstarch
¾ cup port wine
1 cup heavy cream
2 tablespoons confectioners' sugar
¼ cup slivered blanched almonds

Wash the prunes, cover with water and let soak overnight. Bring to a boil, add ½ cup of the sugar, and cook over low heat 25 minutes or until tender. Drain, pit and purée in an electric blender or force through a sieve.

Return the prunes to the saucepan; add the cornstarch mixed with the wine and the remaining sugar. Cook over low heat, stirring steadily, until thickened. Cool.

Whip the cream and fold half of it into the prune mixture. Turn into 6 serving dishes. Mix the remaining whipped cream with the confectioners' sugar and spoon on top. Chill. Sprinkle with the almonds.

Serves 6.

Chinese Meringue-Chestnut Dessert

(PEIPING DUST)

MERINGUE

2 egg whites
¼ teaspoon cream of tartar
⅛ teaspoon salt
⅓ cup sugar
1 teaspoon vanilla extract

Preheat oven to 275°.

Beat the egg whites, cream of tartar and salt until stiff but not dry. Beat in the sugar a tablespoon at a time. Add vanilla. Pipe through a pastry tube into a mound on a baking pan lined with parchment or other paper. Bake 50 minutes or until delicately browned. Remove from the paper and cool.

CHESTNUT MIXTURE

2 pounds chestnuts
3 cups milk
4 tablespoons butter
1 cup sugar
3 tablespoons light rum
¼ cup heavy cream

Cut a crisscross on the pointed ends of each chestnut. Cover them with water, bring to a boil and cook over low heat 10 minutes. Drain and remove the shells. Combine the shelled chestnuts and milk in a saucepan; bring to a boil and cook over low heat 25 minutes or until chestnuts are very tender. Drain and force through a sieve or ricer. Mix in the butter, sugar, rum and cream. Put through a pastry tube, using the smallest nozzle, (or put through a sieve again) onto the meringue. The result should look like very thin noodles. Cover with whipped cream and decorate with candied cherries if desired.

Serves 8–10.

Danish Fruit Dessert

(RODGRODE MED FLODE)

1 quart currants
1 pint raspberries
2 cups water
¾ cup sugar
Potato flour or cornstarch
½ cup blanched slivered almonds
Heavy cream

Wash the currants and raspberries; combine with the water in a saucepan. Bring to a boil and cook over low heat 10 minutes. Force the fruits through a food mill. Mix in the sugar. Measure the juice and return to saucepan. For each cup of juice, use 1 teaspoon potato flour. Mix to a paste with a little water until smooth, then stir into the juice. Cook over low heat, stirring steadily, until thickened and clear. Mix in the almonds and pour into a bowl. Chill. Serve with cream, whipped or liquid.

Serves 6–8.

Chinese Kumquats in Ginger Syrup

1½ pounds kumquats
2 cups water
1 cup sugar
½ cup preserved ground ginger
3 tablespoons lime or lemon juice

Wash the kumquats in warm water; drain and dry. Prick each kumquat with a fork in several places.

Bring the water and sugar to a boil and add the kumquats. Cook over low heat 20 minutes or until syrup is thick and clear. Stir in the ginger and lime or lemon juice. Pack into sterile jars and seal.

Makes about 3 pints.

Chinese Fruits in Syrup

2 tablespoons sugar
4 tablespoons water
2 tablespoons cognac
2 teaspoons lemon juice
1 orange
2 cups fresh or canned pineapple, cubed
1 can lichee nuts, drained

Cook the sugar and water until syrupy; cool and stir in the cognac and lemon juice.

Peel and segment the orange; toss with the pineapple and lichees. Pour the syrup over the fruits; chill 1 hour.

Serves 6–8.

Korean Fruit Cup Dessert

(WHASHAI)

2 cups orange juice
½ cup sugar
½ teaspoon cinnamon
2 tangerines or oranges, peeled and segmented
2 peaches, peeled and sliced
1 cup sliced strawberries or whole raspberries
¼ cup blanched chopped almonds or peanuts

Cook the orange juice, sugar and cinnamon until a syrup is formed. Cool. Combine the fruits in a bowl and pour syrup over them. Chill 1 hour; sprinkle with the nuts and serve in sherbet cups.

Serves 6.

Ice Cream and Sherbets

Strawberry Ice Cream

1 cup sugar
1 cup water
1 tablespoon lemon juice
2 quarts strawberries
1 cup heavy cream

Cook the sugar, water and lemon juice, stirring steadily to the boiling point, then cook 5 minutes longer. Cool.

Purée the berries in an electric blender or force through a sieve. When the syrup is cool, mix it with the berries. Whip the cream and fold it in. Turn into 2 dry refrigerator trays or into a mold. Cover. Freeze until firm.

Serves 6–8.

Coffee Ice Cream

8 egg yolks
2½ cups heavy cream
1 tablespoon instant coffee
¾ cup superfine sugar

Beat the egg yolks in the top of a double boiler. Stir in the cream and coffee. Place over hot water and cook, stirring steadily until thickened, but do not let boil. Remove from the heat, stir in the sugar 1 minute, cool, then strain. Turn into 2 dry refrigerator trays. Freeze in the freezer or refrigerator, with control set at coldest point, until edges set. Turn into a bowl and beat with a rotary beater. Return to trays, cover with foil and freeze until set.

Serves 8–10.

Sicilian Coffee Whip

(GELATO AL CAFFÈE)

2 eggs
½ cup sugar
½ cup light cream
½ cup milk
1 tablespoon instant coffee
⅛ teaspoon salt
1 teaspoon orange extract
1½ cups heavy cream

Beat the eggs in the top of a double boiler with an electric mixer, rotary beater or wire whisk. Beat in the sugar, light cream, milk, coffee and salt. Place over hot water and cook, beating steadily, until thickened. Remove from the heat and stir in the orange extract. Cool, stirring occasionally.

Whip the cream and fold into the coffee mixture. Turn into a 1-quart mold. Cover with a piece of buttered waxed paper, then with the mold cover or aluminum foil. Freeze until firm, about 6 hours or overnight. Unmold onto a chilled serving dish.

Serves 6–8.

Belgian Coffee Ice Cream

(CAFÉ LIÈGEOISE)

2 tablespoons instant coffee
3 tablespoons boiling water
½ cup sugar
¼ cup water
4 egg yolks, beaten
2 cups heavy cream

Dissolve the coffee in the boiling water. Cook the sugar and the ¼ cup water until a thread forms when a fork is dipped into it and lifted. Very gradually add the syrup to the egg yolks, beating constantly until thick. Stir in the coffee.

Whip the cream and fold into the coffee mixture. Turn into an ice tray and place in the freezer until sides become mushy. Remove and beat with a rotary beater 2 minutes. Spoon into tall glasses or sherbet cups and return to the freezer until set.

Serves 6.

French Vanilla Ice Cream

6 egg yolks
⅛ teaspoon salt
¾ cup sugar
3 cups light cream, scalded
1½ cups heavy cream
1 teaspoon powdered vanilla

Beat the egg yolks, salt and sugar in the top of a double boiler until thick and light. Gradually add the scalded light cream, stirring steadily to prevent curdling. Place over hot water and cook, stirring constantly, until mixture coats the spoon. Strain through a fine strainer and chill.

Whip the heavy cream lightly and fold into the egg yolk mixture with the vanilla. Turn into dry refrigerator trays. Freeze, with refrigerator or freezer set at coldest point, until sides begin to set. Turn into a bowl and beat until frothy. Return to trays and freeze again. Beat again and then freeze solid. If ice cream is not to be served immediately, cover trays with foil.

Serves 6–8.

VARIATION

Chocolate Ice Cream: Add 2 ounces melted semi-sweet chocolate to the egg yolk mixture and proceed as directed for French Vanilla Ice Cream.

Cuban Coconut Ice Cream

2 cups flaked coconut
2 cups milk
3 egg yolks
¾ cup sugar
2 cups heavy cream
½ cup packaged fine grated coconut

Mix the flaked coconut and milk in a saucepan. Bring to a boil, remove from heat and let stand 30 minutes. Strain the milk, pressing all the liquid from the coconut; discard coconut.

Beat the egg yolks and sugar in the saucepan; gradually add the coconut milk, stirring steadily to prevent curdling. Cook over low heat, stirring continuously until thickened. Do not let boil. Cool 15 minutes.

Whip the cream and fold it into the yolk mixture with the grated coconut. Turn into dry refrigerator trays and freeze until sides become mushy. Turn into a bowl and beat until frothy; return to trays. Freeze until firm.

Serves 6–8.

Ginger Ice Cream

1½ cups milk
3 cups heavy cream
⅔ cup sugar
5 teaspoons flour
¼ teaspoon salt
2 egg yolks
1 teaspoon vanilla extract
½ cup finely chopped crystallized ginger

Heat the milk and 1½ cups of the cream in the top of a double boiler over direct heat. Mix the sugar, flour and salt; add a little of the hot milk and cream, stirring until smooth. Return to top of double boiler.

Beat the egg yolks lightly; gradually add the hot mixture, stirring steadily to prevent curdling. Return to top of double boiler and place over hot water, stirring continuously until mixture coats the spoon. Remove from heat and stir in the vanilla and ginger. Cool.

Whip the remaining cream and fold into the ginger mixture. Pour into dry refrigerator trays and freeze until sides are firm. Empty into a bowl, and beat with an electric or rotary beater until fluffy. Return to trays and freeze until firm.

Makes about 1½ quarts.

Peach Melba

(PÊCHES MELBA)

3 large firm peaches
1 cup sugar
½ cup water
1 teaspoon vanilla extract
1½ pints vanilla ice cream
Berry Sauce made with raspberries or bottled Melba Sauce

Place the peaches in boiling water for 1 minute. Drain, pull off the skin, cut peaches in half and discard the pits.

Bring the sugar and water to a boil; cook 5 minutes. Add the peaches, and cook over low heat 10 minutes. Mix in the vanilla extract. Let fruit cool in the syrup, then drain. Chill.

For each portion served, place a ball of ice cream on a chilled dish. Put a peach half over it and cover with the raspberry sauce.

Serves 6.

Coffee Parfait

3 cups milk
1½ cups sugar
3 tablespoons instant coffee
6 egg yolks
6 egg whites
1½ cups heavy cream

Cook the milk until bubbles begin to form around the edges. Remove from the heat and mix in the sugar and coffee until dissolved.

Beat the egg yolks in a bowl; gradually add the hot coffee mixture, stirring steadily to prevent curdling. Return to saucepan, and cook over low heat, stirring steadily, until mixture coats the spoon. Cool.

Beat the egg whites until stiff but not dry, and fold into the coffee mixture. Turn into dry refrigerator trays and freeze until edges set. Turn into a bowl and beat with an electric mixer or rotary mixer until fluffy and smooth. Return to trays and freeze until firm.

Whip the cream. Put alternate layers of the coffee mixture and whipped cream into 8 parfait glasses.

Serves 8.

Pineapple Parfait

(PARFAIT D'ANANAS)

6 egg yolks
½ cup sugar
⅓ cup Cointreau (orange liqueur)
2 cups heavy cream
½ cup drained canned crushed pineapple

Beat the egg yolks and sugar in the top of a double boiler. Place over hot water and cook, stirring constantly, until thick and frothy. Remove from heat and stir in the Cointreau. Chill 2 hours.

Whip the cream and fold into the yolk mixture with the pineapple. Spoon into 8 to 10 parfait glasses or sherbet cups. Chill 2 hours before serving.

Serves 8–10.

Pineapple Bombe

(BOMBE AUX ANANAS)

1½ cups finely diced pineapple
⅓ cup Kirsch (cherry liqueur)
1⅛ cups sugar
¾ cup water
6 egg yolks
1 teaspoon vanilla extract
3 cups heavy cream

Soak the pineapple in the liqueur while preparing the custard. Cook the sugar and water over low heat, stirring constantly to the boiling point, then cook 5 minutes or until syrupy.

Beat the egg yolks in the top of a double boiler. Very gradually beat in the syrup. Place over hot water and cook, beating continuously, until thick and creamy. Remove from the heat, mix in the vanilla, and put through a fine strainer. Cool, stirring frequently.

Whip the cream and fold into the custard mixture. Line a chilled 2-quart *bombe* or other mold with half the mixture. Chill 1 hour. Fold the pineapple into the remaining mixture and fill the mold. Cover with a piece of buttered waxed paper, put the lid on and freeze overnight.

To unmold, dip the mold into hot water and turn out onto a chilled serving dish. Decorate with *marrons glacés* (candied chestnuts) or candied fruits.

Serves 10–12.

Frozen Almond Cream

(GELATO DI MANDORLE)

2 eggs
1 tablespoon cornstarch
3 cups light cream
½ cup sugar
⅛ teaspoon salt
2 teaspoons almond extract
½ cup blanched chopped almonds

Beat the eggs with a wire whisk or rotary beater in the top of a double boiler. Mix in the cornstarch until smooth, then the cream, sugar and salt. Place over hot water and cook, beating constantly until thickened, but do not let boil. Remove from heat. Stir in the almond extract; strain. Cool, then mix in the almonds.

Turn into a buttered melon mold. Place a piece of buttered waxed paper over the top, then cover mold. Place in freezer section of the refrigerator or home freezer. Freeze 4 hours or until firm. To unmold, hold a hot towel around the mold or dip bottom quickly into hot water, then turn out onto a chilled serving dish.

Serves 6–8.

Coffee Spumoni

(SPUMONI AL CAFFÈE)

1 tablespoon instant coffee
2 tablespoons hot water
8 egg whites
7 tablespoons sugar
1¼ cups heavy cream, whipped

Dissolve the coffee in the water and cool. Beat the egg whites until stiff but not dry. Gradually beat in the sugar until mixture is very stiff and glossy. Beat in the coffee, and fold in the whipped cream. Turn into a 2 to 3 quart mold. Place in the freezing compartment of the refrigerator or home freezer until frozen.

Serves 8–10.

Biscuit Tortoni

1 cup heavy cream
5 tablespoons superfine sugar
1 egg white, stiffly beaten
½ cup ground, blanched toasted almonds
1 tablespoon Strega (orange liqueur)

Whip the cream until it begins to hold its shape, then beat in the sugar. Fold in the egg white, almonds and Strega. Divide the mixture among 8 2-inch paper cups. Place in the freezer or freezing compartment of the refrigerator until firm.

Serves 8.

Note: Additional ground almonds may be sprinkled on top.

Chocolate Chip Tortoni

2 egg yolks
½ cup sugar
¼ cup boiling water
1 cup heavy cream, whipped
1 cup semi-sweet chocolate bits
2 tablespoons butter
2 egg whites
2 teaspoons vanilla extract
¼ cup chopped blanched toasted almonds

Beat the egg yolks and ¼ cup of the sugar until thick and light. Gradually beat in the boiling water. Cool. Fold in the whipped cream. Turn into a dry refrigerator tray and freeze until just set.

Melt the chocolate and butter over hot water.

Beat the egg whites until stiff but not dry. Gradually beat in the remaining sugar until mixture is very stiff and glossy. Stir in the vanilla.

Turn the frozen mixture into a bowl, and stir it quickly until smooth but not melted. Quickly but gradually, stir in the chocolate, making a marbled effect. Fold in the meringue and nuts. Spoon into 16 2-ounce paper cups. Freeze until firm.

Makes 16.

Sicilian Ice Cream Dessert

(CASSATA)

½ cup chopped candied fruits
2 tablespoons Strega (orange liqueur)
1 quart vanilla ice cream
1 pint chocolate ice cream
¾ cup heavy cream
¼ cup superfine sugar
1 egg white, beaten stiff

Combine the fruits and Strega; let stand 15 minutes, mixing frequently. Let the ice cream soften. Dip a large spoon in warm water and spread the vanilla ice cream on the bottom and sides of a 1½-quart round mold. Spread the chocolate ice cream over it, leaving center hollow. Freeze 30 minutes.

Whip the cream, mix in the sugar, then fold in the fruits and the egg white. Fill the center of the mold with the mixture and level off the top with a knife. Cover with a piece of buttered waxed paper and then with the cover of the mold or a piece of aluminum foil. Freeze until very firm. Unmold and cut into wedges.

Serves 6–8.

Sherbets

LEMON

¾ cup sugar
⅓ cup lemon juice
Dash salt
2 cups milk

PINEAPPLE

½ cup sugar
2 tablespoons lemon juice
Dash salt
½ cup frozen concentrated pineapple juice
1½ cups milk

BERRY

2 cups puréed strawberries or raspberries
2 tablespoons lemon juice
¾ cup sugar
Dash salt
2 cups milk

The method of preparing all sherbets is the same. Mix together all the ingredients but the milk. Gradually stir in the milk. Turn into dry refrigerator trays and freeze until edges are firm. Empty into a bowl and beat with an electric mixer or rotary beater until fluffy and smooth. Return to trays and freeze until firm.

Makes about 1 quart.

Rich Lemon Sherbet

1¼ cups sugar
1⅓ cups lemon juice
Dash salt
2 cups milk
2 cups light cream
2 tablespoons grated lemon rind

Mix the sugar, lemon juice and salt until sugar dissolves. Gradually stir in the milk and cream. Pour into dry refrigerator trays. Freeze until edges are firm. Turn into a bowl and beat with an electric mixer or rotary beater until fluffy and smooth. Return to trays. Repeat freezing and beating once more, then freeze until firm.

Makes about 2 quarts.

Buttermilk Sherbet

1 quart buttermilk
½ cup sugar
1½ cups light corn syrup
½ cup lemon juice
2 tablespoons grated lemon rind

Mix all the ingredients together. Pour into 2 dry refrigerator trays. Freeze until edges are firm. Turn into a bowl and beat with an electric mixer or rotary beater until frothy and smooth. Return to trays. Repeat freezing and beating twice more; then freeze until firm.

Makes about 1½ quarts.

Coffee Ice

(GRANITA DE CAFFÈE)

1 cup sugar
1 cup water
3 cups cold double-strength brewed coffee

Combine the sugar and water in a saucepan; bring to a boil and cook over medium heat 5 minutes. Cool; mix with the coffee. Pour into a dry refrigerator tray and freeze without stirring until granular. Serve in sherbet glasses with whipped cream on top.

Serves 4.

Banana Ice

(GRANITA DI BANANA)

1 cup water
1 cup sugar
1½ cups mashed bananas
¾ cup orange juice
2 tablespoons lemon juice

Cook the water and sugar, stirring constantly to the boiling point; then cook 5 minutes longer or until syrupy. Cool.

Mix together the bananas, orange juice and lemon juice. Gradually mix in the syrup. Pour into a dry refrigerator tray. Freeze until sides turn mushy, then turn into a bowl and beat with an electric or rotary beater until fluffy. Return to ice tray and freeze until firm, stirring occasionally.

Serves 4.

Port Wine Ice

3 cups water
1 cup sugar
Dash salt
2 cups port wine
2 tablespoons lemon juice

Bring the water, sugar and salt to a boil; stir constantly. Cook over high heat until syrupy (about 5 minutes). Mix in the port wine and lemon juice. Cool.

Turn into dry refrigerator trays and freeze until sides become mushy. Empty into a bowl and beat with an electric mixer or rotary beater until frothy. Return to trays. Repeat freezing and beating 3 times more, then freeze until firm.

Serves 4–6.

Quick Section—Cakes and Pies Prepared with Mixes

Chocolate Party Cake

1 package chocolate cake mix

1 package instant chocolate pudding

¼ cup vegetable oil

Preheat oven to 350°. Grease a 9-inch tube pan and dust lightly with flour.

Prepare cake mix as package directs, but use 2 extra eggs. Add the instant chocolate pudding and oil. Beat with an electric or rotary beater for 2 minutes. Turn into the pan; bake 45 minutes or until a cake tester comes out clean. Cool on a cake rack 10 minutes before removing cake from pan. Finish cooling on the cake rack. The cake may be split and filled and covered with any frosting or whipped cream, or served plain.

Applesauce Cake

1 package butterscotch cake mix
½ cup canned applesauce
½ cup chopped walnuts or pecans
½ teaspoon cinnamon
¼ teaspoon nutmeg

Prepare cake mix as package directs, but reduce water to 1 cup. Mix in the applesauce, nuts, cinnamon and nutmeg. Bake in two 9-inch layer cake pans. Cool. Frost with Seven-Minute Frosting or whipped cream.

Nut Cake

1 package yellow cake mix
¾ cup ground nuts
1 teaspoon vanilla extract

Prepare cake mix as package directs. Stir in the nuts and vanilla. Bake in two 9-inch layer cake pans. Cool. Frost with Butter Cream Frosting and decorate with nut halves of the variety used in the cake.

Coconut Cake

1 package white cake mix
1½ cups fine grated coconut
½ teaspoon vanilla extract
1½ cups heavy cream
2 tablespoons sugar

Prepare cake mix as package directs, but fold in ¾ cup coconut and the vanilla. Bake in two 8-inch layer cake pans. Cool. Whip the cream and sugar. Spread some between the layers and sprinkle with ½ cup coconut. Cover cake with whipped cream and sprinkle with the remaining coconut. Chill 1 hour.

Lemon-Cognac Cake

1 package lemon custard angel food cake mix
1 cup heavy cream
2 tablespoons confectioners' sugar
¼ cup cognac
¼ cup candied cherries

Prepare and bake cake mix in a 10-inch tube pan as package directs. Cool on a cake rack 15 minutes, then remove from pan. Finish cooling on the rack.

Whip the cream and sugar, then fold in the cognac. Cover the cake with it and decorate with the cherries.

Spice Log

1 package spice cake mix
½ cup confectioners' sugar
1 cup heavy cream, whipped
Butter Cream Frosting
Shaved sweet chocolate

Preheat oven to 350°. Oil an 11-by-16-inch jelly roll pan, line it with waxed paper, leaving a 2-inch piece extending at each end, and grease the paper.

Prepare the cake mix as package directs. Pour three-quarters of the mixture into the lined pan and spread it evenly. (Bake excess batter in a small pan or make cupcakes.) Bake 20 minutes.

Sprinkle the confectioners' sugar on a large piece of waxed paper. Turn cake out onto it. Carefully peel off the paper in which the cake was baked. Roll up the cake lengthwise. Cool 1 hour. Unroll cake and spread with the whipped cream. Reroll cake and cover with the butter cream. Draw a fork over the frosting to mark it like bark. Sprinkle with the chocolate. Chill.

Nun's Torte

1 package yellow cake mix
2 egg whites
⅓ cup sugar
¾ cup sliced blanched almonds
1 cup heavy cream

Preheat oven to 350°.

Prepare the cake mix as package directs. Divide batter between two 9-inch layer cake pans. Beat the egg whites until soft peaks are formed, then gradually beat in the sugar until stiff. Spread over the batter to within ½-inch of the outside edge. Sprinkle meringue with the almonds. Bake 40 minutes or until delicately browned and cake shrinks away from the sides of the pans. Cool on a cake rack 30 minutes, then turn out meringue-side up. Cool 2 hours longer.

Whip the cream and spread over one layer. Cover with the remaining layer, meringue-side up.

Cocoa Surprise Cake

1 package devil's food cake mix
2 cups heavy cream
¼ cup sugar
⅛ teaspoon salt
¼ cup unsweetened cocoa

Prepare and bake mix as package directs in a 9-inch square pan. Cool. Cut a 1-inch piece, horizontally, off the top. Carefully hollow out the inside. Combine the cream, sugar, salt and cocoa; chill 1 hour, then whip. Fill the hollow with half the cream, replace top and cover with the remaining cream. Chill before serving.

Pecan Custard Pie

Pastry for 1-crust pie
1 cup dark corn syrup
1 package vanilla instant pudding
¾ cup light cream
1 egg, beaten
1 cup chopped pecans

Preheat oven to 325°. Line a 9-inch pie plate with the pastry. Gradually stir the corn syrup into the pudding mix, then add the cream and egg. Mix until smooth. Stir in the pecans. Turn into the lined pie plate. Bake 50 minutes or until a cake tester comes out clean.

Refrigerator Lemon Cheese Pie

½ pound cream cheese
2 cups sour cream
1 package instant lemon pudding
1 teaspoon vanilla extract
1 chilled 9-inch Graham Cracker Shell

Beat the cheese until soft, then gradually mix in half the sour cream. Add the pudding mix, vanilla and remaining sour cream, beating with an electric mixer or rotary beater until very smooth and fluffy. Turn into the lined pie plate. Chill until set, about 2 hours.

Frostings, Creams, Custards, Glazes, Fillings and Sauces

Seven-Minute Frosting

2 egg whites
1/8 teaspoon salt
1 1/2 cups sugar
1/2 cup cold water
1 tablespoon light corn syrup
1 1/2 teaspoons vanilla extract

In the top of a double boiler, combine the egg whites, salt, sugar, water and corn syrup. Place over boiling water. Beat with an electric mixer or rotary beater 7 minutes or until stiff peaks form. Turn into a bowl and beat in the vanilla for 1 minute or until thick enough to spread.

Makes about 5 1/2 cups; enough for two layers, a 9-inch square cake or 2 dozen cupcakes.

VARIATIONS

Coffee: Add 1 tablespoon instant coffee to unbeaten mixture. Proceed as directed.

Chocolate: Add 2 tablespoons unsweetened cocoa to unbeaten mixture. Proceed as directed.

Cherry: Add 3 tablespoons maraschino cherry juice to unbeaten mixture. Proceed as directed.

Orange: Substitute 2 teaspoons orange extract for the vanilla. Add 1 tablespoon grated orange rind.

Lemon: Substitute 2 teaspoons lemon extract for the vanilla. Add 2 teaspoons grated lemon rind.

Brown Sugar: Substitute 1½ cups firmly packed brown sugar for the granulated sugar. Proceed as directed.

Rich Chocolate Frosting

5 squares (ounces) unsweetened chocolate
2¼ cups sifted confectioners' sugar
¼ cup hot light cream
1 egg
6 tablespoons soft butter

Break up the chocolate and melt it over hot water. Beat in the confectioners' sugar and cream. Add the egg, beating until smooth and shiny. Add 1 tablespoon butter at a time, beating after each addition until absorbed.

Makes about 2 cups, enough for two layers, a 9-inch square cake or 18 cupcakes.

Butter Cream Frosting

¼ pound (1 stick) butter
4 cups sifted confectioners' sugar
1 egg
⅛ teaspoon salt
1 teaspoon vanilla extract
2 tablespoons light cream

Cream the butter until soft and fluffy; add half the confectioners' sugar very gradually, beating well after each addition. Blend in the egg, salt and vanilla. Add the remaining sugar alternately with the cream, beating until smooth after each addition. It may not be necessary to add all the sugar to obtain the right consistency for spreading.

Makes about 2½ cups, enough for two layers, two 9-inch square cakes or 36 cupcakes.

VARIATIONS

Coffee Butter Cream: Add 1 tablespoon instant coffee when adding the egg.

Chocolate Butter Cream: Add 3 squares melted unsweetened chocolate with the first addition of sugar. Increase cream to 4 tablespoons.

Orange Butter Cream: Substitute 2 tablespoons orange juice for the cream, omit vanilla and add 1 tablespoon finely grated orange rind.

Chocolate Cream Cheese Frosting

½ pound sweet chocolate
¼ teaspoon salt
2 3-ounce packages cream cheese
2 tablespoons light cream
2 cups sifted confectioners' sugar
1 teaspoon vanilla extract

Break the chocolate into small pieces and add the salt. Place over hot water until melted. Cool 10 minutes, then beat in the cream cheese and cream. Gradually beat in the confectioners' sugar, then the vanilla.

Makes about 2 cups, enough for two layers, a 9-inch square cake or 24 cupcakes.

Cream Frosting

4 cups sifted confectioners' sugar
½ cup melted butter
1 teaspoon vanilla extract
1½ cups heavy cream

Mix the confectioners' sugar, butter and vanilla together. Gradually mix in just enough of the cream to make a spreadable mixture. It may not be necessary to add all the cream.

Enough for three 8-inch layers, two 9-inch layers or two 8-inch square cakes.

Pastry Cream

(CRÈME PÂTISSIÈRE)

½ cup flour
1 tablespoon cornstarch
¾ cup sugar
6 egg yolks, beaten
3 cups milk, scalded
1 teaspoon vanilla extract

Sift the flour, cornstarch and sugar into a saucepan. Stir in the egg yolks until smooth. Gradually add the hot milk, stirring steadily to prevent curdling. Cook over low heat, mixing steadily, until thickened. Cool. For a richer cream, 1 cup whipped cream can be folded in. Use for filling cream puffs or napoleons.

Tahitian Coconut Cream

2 envelopes (2 tablespoons) gelatin
⅓ cup cold water
1 cup milk
1 cup sugar
¼ teaspoon salt
1 teaspoon vanilla extract
2 cups heavy cream
1½ cups packaged fine grated coconut

Soften the gelatin in the water. Bring the milk to a boil, remove from the heat and immediately stir in the gelatin, sugar and salt until dissolved. Chill until mixture just begins to set. Don't let it get too firm. Mix in the vanilla.

Whip the cream and fold in with the coconut. Rinse a 9-inch ring mold with cold water and pour the mixture into it. Chill until firm. Carefully unmold onto a serving dish and fill the center with fruits.

Serves 6–8.

Chestnut Cream

(MONT BLANC AUX MARRONS)

2 pounds fresh chestnuts or 1½ pounds dried
2 cups milk
⅓ cup water
¼ teaspoon lemon juice
1 cup sugar
2 teaspoons vanilla extract
3 tablespoons butter
2 cups heavy cream

Cut a crisscross on the pointed end of each fresh chestnut. Cover with water, bring to a boil and cook 5 minutes. Drain and remove the shells. If dried chestnuts are used, cover with water, bring to a boil, remove from heat and let soak 1 hour. Drain.

Combine the chestnuts and milk in a saucepan. Bring to a boil and cook over low heat 25 minutes or until tender. Drain and purée in an electric blender, or force through a sieve or ricer. Be sure the purée is very smooth.

Cook the water, lemon juice, sugar and vanilla until a thread is formed when a fork is raised from the pan. Gradually add to the chestnuts, mixing steadily. Beat in the butter. Cool 10 minutes.

Butter a 9-inch ring mold or a 1-quart round dish and dust it with sugar. Force the chestnut mixture through a pastry tube (using a round end) or pile onto the dish. Immediately unmold onto a serving dish. Chill 2 hours. Whip the cream and fill the center of the ring or pile on top of the mound.

Serves 6–8.

Strawberry Cream

2 envelopes (2 tablespoons) gelatin
⅓ cup cold water
1 quart strawberries
1 cup sugar
3 cups heavy cream
¼ cup Kirsch or other fruit liqueur

Soften the gelatin in the water, then place over hot water and stir until dissolved. Wash, hull and dry the berries. Reserve 8 to 10 berries for garnish. Toss the remaining berries with ½ cup of the sugar.

Whip the cream, then beat in the sugar and liqueur. The cream should be fairly firm. Fold in the gelatin thoroughly.

In a 3-quart mold or bowl, arrange as many alternate layers of the sugared berries and cream as possible. Chill overnight. Unmold or serve directly from the dish, garnished with the reserved berries. (Pour off any juices that may have gathered on the bottom.) Serve with Strawberry Sauce if desired.

Serves 8–10.

Note: Raspberries may be prepared in the same manner.

Mocha Cream

(CREMA AL MOKA)

1 tablespoon instant coffee
1 tablespoon unsweetened cocoa
½ cup boiling water
4 egg yolks
¾ cup sugar
2 tablespoons dark rum
1 cup heavy cream, whipped

Dissolve the coffee and cocoa in the boiling water. Beat the egg yolks in the top of a double boiler. Beat in the sugar. Add the hot cocoa mixture, beating continuously. Place over hot water and cook, stirring constantly, until thickened.

Remove from the heat and beat until cold. Stir in the rum, then fold in the whipped cream. Turn into a 1½-quart mold and freeze.

Serves 6–8.

Mocha Custard Cream

(CRÈME SAINT-HONORÉ AU MOKA)

5 egg yolks
1⅛ cups sugar
⅔ cup sifted flour
2 cups milk, scalded
1 tablespoon butter
2 teaspoons vanilla extract
2 teaspoons instant coffee
8 egg whites
⅛ teaspoon salt

Beat the egg yolks; gradually beat in 1 cup of the sugar until thick and light. Beat in the flour. Gradually add the hot milk, stirring steadily to prevent curdling. Cook over low heat, beating continuously, until thick and smooth. Remove from the heat and mix in the butter, vanilla and coffee.

Beat the egg whites and salt until soft peaks form, then beat in the remaining sugar until meringue is stiff. Mix one fourth of the meringue into the hot custard, then fold in the rest. Pour into a serving dish and chill.

Serves 6–8.

Coffee Butter Cream Dessert

(CREMA DI BURRO AL CAFFÈE)

1 tablespoon instant coffee
½ cup hot water
½ pound butter
1 cup sugar
2 egg yolks
2 cups heavy cream, whipped
16 ladyfingers

Dissolve the coffee in the water; cool. Cream the butter and sugar until light and fluffy. Beat in the egg yolks and coffee until smooth, then fold in the whipped cream.

Split the ladyfingers lengthwise. Arrange alternate layers of the ladyfingers and the coffee mixture in a buttered mold. Start and end with the ladyfingers. Freeze until firm, then carefully unmold.

Serves 6–8.

Note: Very thin spongecake layers may be used in place of the ladyfingers.

Vanilla Bavarian Cream

(BAVAROIS VANILLE)

1 envelope (1 tablespoon) gelatin
3 tablespoons cold water
4 egg yolks
½ cup powdered sugar
1 cup milk, scalded
1 teaspoon vanilla extract
1 cup heavy cream, whipped

Soften the gelatin in the water. Beat the egg yolks with a wire whisk or rotary beater in the top of a double boiler; add the sugar, beating until thick and light. Gradually add the hot milk, stirring continuously to prevent curdling. Place over hot water and cook, stirring constantly, until it thickens and mixture coats the spoon. Stir in the gelatin until dissolved, then the vanilla. Cool, stirring occasionally. When cold, fold in the whipped cream.

Turn into a 1½-quart mold or individual molds and chill until set.

Serves 6–8.

VARIATIONS

Chocolate Bavarian Cream (BAVAROIS CHOCOLAT): Melt 2 squares (2 ounces) unsweetened chocolate in 2 tablespoons brewed coffee. Add to the yolk mixture when adding the gelatin. Proceed as directed.

Ginger Bavarian Cream (BAVAROIS GINGEMBRE): Add ½ cup finely chopped preserved ginger to the Vanilla Bavarian Cream.

Almond Cream

(CRÈME FRANGIPANE)

1 egg
1 egg yolk
¾ cup sugar
⅓ cup sifted flour
1 cup milk, scalded
3 tablespoons butter
½ teaspoon almond extract
½ cup finely ground almonds

Beat the egg and egg yolk in a saucepan; gradually beat in the sugar until pale and thick. Beat in the flour. Very gradually add the hot milk, mixing steadily. Cook over low heat, beating steadily, until smooth and thick. Beat constantly with a wooden spoon so that mixture doesn't scorch on the bottom.

Remove from heat and beat in the butter, almond extract and almonds. Use as a filling for crêpes or tarts.

Almond Cream, French Style

(BLANCMANGE)

1¼ cups blanched almonds
2 cups milk
1½ envelopes (1½ tablespoons) gelatin
¼ cup water
1 cup light cream
½ cup sugar
½ teaspoon almond extract

An electric blender will simplify the preparation. Put a little more than ¼ cup of the almonds at a time into the blender bowl. Run machine until almonds are very fine, then add ½ cup milk. Strain through a fine sieve. Repeat with balance. If you haven't a blender, grind the almonds very fine, then pound in a mortar with pestle, gradually adding the milk. Strain.

Soften the gelatin in the water. Combine the cream, sugar and almond-milk mixture in a saucepan. Bring just to a boil, stirring constantly. Immediately remove from the heat and stir in the gelatin until dissolved. Mix in the almond extract. Pour into a lightly oiled 7-inch ring mold and chill until set.

Carefully unmold onto a chilled serving dish and fill the center with sweetened strawberries or raspberries.

Serves 4–6.

Rich Cheese Dessert

(CREMA DI FORMAGGIO)

1½ pounds cream cheese, softened
¾ cup sugar
6 egg yolks, beaten
3 tablespoons heavy cream
3 tablespoons cognac
Raspberries or strawberries

Beat the cheese in an electric mixer or blender until very smooth. Beat in the sugar until smooth; add the egg yolks, cream and cognac, beating until very smooth and thick. Pour into a serving dish and chill. Garnish with raspberries or strawberries.

Serves 8–10.

Chocolate Whipped Cream

1 cup heavy cream
1 tablespoon sugar
2 tablespoons sifted unsweetened cocoa

Whip the cream until it begins to thicken, then beat in the sugar and cocoa until whipped.

Makes 2 cups.

Coffee Whipped Cream

2 cups (one pint) heavy cream
1 tablespoon instant coffee
¼ cup confectioners' sugar

Place cream in a chilled bowl. Beat until cream begins to thicken. Gradually sprinkle in coffee and sugar, continuing to beat until cream is stiff.

Spanish Custard

(FLAN)

1¾ cups sugar
¼ cup water
3 eggs
½ teaspoon salt
3 cups milk, scalded
1 teaspoon vanilla extract

Preheat oven to 325°.

Combine 1 cup sugar and the water in a saucepan. Cook over low heat until light brown. Divide among six buttered custard cups, or pour into a 1-quart buttered mold.

Beat the eggs lightly. Mix in the remaining sugar and the salt. Gradually add the hot milk, stirring constantly to prevent curdling. Add the vanilla. Pour into the prepared cups or mold.

Place in a shallow pan of warm water. Bake the individual cups 35 minutes, large one 55 minutes, or until a knife inserted in the center comes out clean. Cool. Carefully unmold. Serve very cold.

Serves 6.

Glazed Custard

(CRÈME BRÛLÉE)

6 egg yolks
⅓ cup granulated sugar
3 cups heavy cream, scalded
2 teaspoons vanilla extract
½ cup firmly packed brown sugar

Preheat oven to 325°.

Beat the egg yolks and granulated sugar in a bowl until light and smooth. Gradually beat in the cream, then mix in the vanilla. Strain into a 1½-quart baking dish. Place in a shallow pan of hot water. Bake 35 minutes or until a knife inserted in the center comes out clean. Cool, then chill.

Just before serving, spread the brown sugar over the custard.

Place the dish on a board or over cracked ice. Place under a hot broiler until sugar melts completely. *Crème brûlée* may be served hot or very cold.

Serves 6–8.

Caramel Custard Cream

(CRÈME RENVERSÉE AU CARAMEL)

CARAMEL

2 *tablespoons water*
½ *cup sugar*

Cook the water and sugar in a saucepan until caramel colored. Immediately pour into a 9-inch ring mold, turning the mold to coat the sides.

CUSTARD CREAM

3 *eggs*
3 *egg yolks*
½ *cup sugar*
1 *teaspoon vanilla extract*
1 *cup heavy cream and 1½ cups milk, scalded together*

Preheat oven to 325°.

Beat the eggs and egg yolks in a bowl; gradually beat in the sugar and vanilla until thick and light. Very gradually beat in the hot cream and milk mixture, stirring steadily to prevent curdling. Strain into the mold. Set the mold in a shallow pan and add enough hot water to reach halfway up the side of the mold.

Bake 40 minutes or until a knife inserted in the center comes out clean. Remove from pan of water.

Chill. To unmold, run a spatula around the edge, place a plate over the custard, turn upside down (plate will now be on the bottom) and remove the mold. Serve with lightly whipped cream.

Serves 6–8.

Viennese Chilled Custard with Cherries

(KIRSCHENCREME)

1 pound Bing cherries, pitted, or 2 cups canned, drained
3/4 cup Kirsch (cherry liqueur)
4 egg yolks
1/2 cup sugar
1 cup light cream, heated
1/2 cup heavy cream, whipped

Marinate the cherries in 1/2 cup of the Kirsch while preparing the custard.

Beat the egg yolks and sugar in the top of a double boiler until light and thick. Gradually beat in the hot cream. Place over hot water and cook, mixing steadily, until mixture coats the spoon. Cool, then chill 30 minutes. Fold in the whipped cream and remaining Kirsch. Spoon into 6 to 8 sherbet glasses and chill again. Serve the marinated cherries as a sauce.

Serves 6–8.

Vanilla Custard

6 egg yolks
4 tablespoons sugar
2 cups heavy cream
1 teaspoon vanilla extract

Preheat oven to 325°.

Beat the egg yolks until light. Heat the sugar and cream until the sugar dissolves. Gradually add to the egg yolks, stirring constantly to prevent curdling. Mix in the vanilla. Strain into 8 custard cups; place in a shallow pan of hot water. Bake 15 minutes or until a silver knife inserted in the center comes out clean. Cool then chill.

Serves 8.

Mocha Custard

3 ounces sweet chocolate
2 tablespoons brewed coffee
6 egg yolks
2 tablespoons sugar
2 cups heavy cream, scalded

Preheat oven to 325°.

Melt the chocolate in the coffee over low heat. Cool. Beat the egg yolks and sugar together until light. Mix in the chocolate, then very gradually the hot cream. Spoon into 8 custard cups; place in a shallow pan of hot water. Bake 15 minutes or until a silver knife inserted in the center comes out clean. Cool then chill.

Serves 8.

French Vanilla Custard

(POT DE CRÈME VANILLE)

6 egg yolks
2 cups heavy cream
4 tablespoons sugar
1 teaspoon vanilla extract

Preheat oven to 325°.

There are special French *pots* (small pottery cups) available, but if you don't have them, use small custard cups.

Beat the egg yolks in a bowl. Heat the cream and sugar, then add to the egg yolks, beating steadily to prevent curdling. Stir in the vanilla.

Strain into 8 cups; set in a shallow pan of water. Bake 15 minutes or until a silver knife inserted in the center comes out clean. Cool, then chill.

Serves 8.

French Chocolate Custard

(POT DE CRÈME AU CHOCOLAT)

3 ounces sweet chocolate
2 tablespoons brewed coffee
6 egg yolks
2 tablespoons sugar
2 cups heavy cream, heated

Preheat oven to 325°.

Break the chocolate into small pieces and combine with the coffee. Let melt over very low heat. Cool. Beat the egg yolks, sugar and chocolate together. Gradually add the cream, stirring steadily to prevent curdling. Pour into 8 *pots* or custard cups. Set in a shallow pan of hot water. Bake 15 minutes or until a silver knife inserted in the center comes clean. Cool, then chill.

Serves 8.

Frozen Coffee Custard

(CREMA FREDDA AL CAFFÈE)

1 tablespoon instant coffee
2 tablespoons hot water
6 egg yolks
¼ cup sugar
¼ teaspoon salt
¼ cup flour
1½ cups milk, scalded
1 teaspoon vanilla extract

Dissolve the coffee in the hot water. Beat the egg yolks in a saucepan. Mix in the sugar, salt and flour until smooth. Gradually add the hot milk, stirring steadily to prevent curdling. Cook over low heat, stirring constantly, until mixture coats the spoon. Remove from heat and mix in the vanilla and coffee. Immediately strain into a 1-quart mold. Freeze until firm. Serve with ladyfingers if desired.

Serves 4–6.

Marsala Custard

(ZABAGLIONE)

8 egg yolks
½ cup fine granulated sugar
1 cup Marsala or sweet sherry

Zabaglione may be prepared at the table. Use a chafing dish or an attractive double boiler. In the top part, beat the egg yolks and sugar with a wire whisk until thick. Beat in the wine; place over hot water and beat until hot, very thick and frothy. Do not let boil. Spoon into tall glasses or sherbet cups and serve immediately with ladyfingers if desired.

Serves 6–8.

Neapolitan Custard

(CREMA NAPOLETANA)

3 egg yolks
¼ cup sugar
2 tablespoons cornstarch
2 cups light cream, heated
1 tablespoon Strega (orange liqueur)

Beat the egg yolks with a wire whisk or rotary beater in the top of a double boiler. Beat in the sugar until thick, then blend in the cornstarch. Gradually add the hot cream, stirring steadily to prevent curdling. Place over hot water and cook, beating constantly until thick. Remove from heat. Beat in the Strega until mixture is glossy. Spoon into 6 custard or sherbet cups. Chill.

Serves 6.

Indian Custard Pudding

2 cups milk
2 cups light cream
1/3 cup yellow cornmeal
1 1/2 teaspoons salt
1/2 cup firmly packed brown sugar
3/4 cup molasses
1/4 teaspoon mace
1/2 teaspoon powdered ginger
3 tablespoons butter
2 eggs
1 cup heavy cream
1 teaspoon vanilla extract

Preheat oven to 300°.

Combine the milk and 1 1/2 cups of the light cream in the top of a double boiler. Bring to a boil over direct heat. Mix the cornmeal, salt and remaining light cream until smooth. Gradually stir into the hot liquid. Place over hot water, stirring very frequently until thickened (about 20 minutes). Beat in the brown sugar, molasses, mace, ginger and butter.

Beat the eggs in a bowl, gradually add the hot mixture, stirring steadily to prevent curdling. Turn into a buttered 2-quart baking dish. Pour the heavy cream mixed with the vanilla over the top. Place the dish in a shallow pan of hot water. Bake 40 minutes or until a knife inserted in the center comes out clean. Cool, then chill.

Serves 6–8.

Banana Custard

3 eggs
1/4 cup sugar
2 tablespoons flour
2 cups milk
2 tablespoons cognac
1 cup thinly sliced bananas

Preheat oven to 400°.

Beat the eggs and sugar until light and fluffy. Mix the flour with a little of the milk until smooth, then add to the egg mixture with the rest of the milk. Mix well and strain. Stir in the cognac and bananas. Turn into a buttered 1-quart baking dish. Set the dish in a pan of hot water. Bake 40 minutes or until a knife inserted in the center comes out clean. Serve very cold.

Serves 4–6.

Floating Island

(OEUFS À LA NEIGE)

6 egg whites
1/8 teaspoon salt
1 cup powdered sugar
1 cup light cream
1 cup milk
2 tablespoons granulated sugar
1 teaspoon vanilla extract
6 egg yolks

Beat the egg whites and salt until soft peaks form. Very gradually beat in the powdered sugar until mixture is very stiff.

In a saucepan, bring just to a boil the cream, milk and granulated sugar. Stir in the vanilla. Pick up the meringue by the tablespoon and gently mold into egg shapes with the aid of another spoon. Drop into the boiling mixture and cook over low heat 2 minutes; turn with a fork and cook 2 minutes longer. Remove the meringue with a slotted spoon and let drain on a rack.

Strain the milk mixture. Beat the egg yolks in a bowl; gradually add the hot milk mixture, stirring steadily to prevent curdling. Return to the saucepan and cook over low heat stirring steadily until slightly thickened. Do not let boil. Pour into a bowl and chill. Just before serving, float the meringues on top. A raspberry or strawberry may be placed in the center of each meringue if desired.

Serves 6–8.

VARIATION

Meringues in Chocolate Custard (BOULES AU CHOCOLAT): When preparing the custard, add ½ cup unsweetened cocoa and ½ cup more sugar to the egg yolks, then proceed as directed above.

Curaçao Pumpkin Custard

2 eggs
½ cup firmly packed brown sugar
½ teaspoon salt
¼ teaspoon nutmeg
¼ teaspoon powdered ginger
1 cup cooked or canned puréed pumpkin
1 cup heavy cream
1 tablespoon cognac
2 tablespoons grated orange rind

Preheat oven to 325°.

Beat the eggs, sugar, salt, nutmeg and ginger until thick and light. Mix in the pumpkin, then the cream, cognac and orange rind. Pour into 6 buttered custard cups. Set the cups in a shallow pan of hot water. Bake 40 minutes or until a knife inserted in the center comes out clean. Remove the cups from the pan. Serve warm or cold, with ginger-flavored whipped cream.

Serves 6.

Chocolate Glaze

¼ pound sweet chocolate
3 tablespoons water
1 tablespoon butter
1 cup sifted confectioners' sugar
⅛ teaspoon salt
¾ teaspoon vanilla extract

Break the chocolate into small pieces; combine in a saucepan with the water and butter. Cook over very low heat until melted and smooth. Sift the confectioners' sugar and salt into a bowl; gradually mix in the melted chocolate. Stir in the vanilla. Cool until thick enough to spread.

Makes about ¾ cup, enough for the top of a 10-inch tube cake or a layer cake.

Mocha Glaze

2 tablespoons unsweetened cocoa
1 teaspoon instant coffee
3 tablespoons hot water
2 tablespoons soft butter
1½ cups sifted confectioners' sugar

Mix together the cocoa, coffee, water and butter until smooth. Gradually beat in the confectioners' sugar until smooth and spreadable.

Makes enough for the top of a layer cake, an 8-inch square cake, 3 dozen cookies or 2 dozen cupcakes.

Apricot Glaze

1 cup apricot preserves
2 tablespoons cognac or fruit liqueur

Makes 1 cup.

Force the preserves through a sieve into a saucepan. Bring to a boil and stir in the liqueur. Use while warm.

Orange Glaze

1 tablespoon butter
1 tablespoon milk
1¼ cups sifted confectioners' sugar
1½ tablespoons orange juice
2 teaspoons grated orange rind

Heat the butter and milk together until butter melts. Stir in the sugar until smooth. Beat in the orange juice and rind. Cool until thick enough to spread.

Makes about ⅔ cup, enough to glaze the top of a 10-inch tube cake or layer cake.

VARIATION

Lemon Glaze: Substitute lemon juice and rind for the orange juice and rind.

Walnut Butter Cream Filling

1¼ cups ground walnuts
2 tablespoons cognac
1 egg white
4 tablespoons sugar
¾ cup (1½ sticks) softened butter

Mix the walnuts and cognac. Combine the egg white and sugar in the top of a double boiler; place over hot water and beat until the consistency of heavy cream. Mix in the walnuts and then gradually beat in the butter. Spread between cake layers or use as a filling for a cake roll.

Orange Cream Filling

2 tablespoons cornstarch
¾ cup sugar
2 egg yolks, lightly beaten
1 egg white, lightly beaten
⅔ cup orange juice
1 tablespoon butter
2 teaspoons grated orange rind

Mix together all the ingredients but the orange rind in a saucepan. Cook over low heat, stirring constantly until thickened (about 5 minutes). Remove from heat and mix in the orange rind. Cool.

Makes about 1¼ cups, enough to fill two layers.

VARIATION

Lemon Cream Filling: Substitute 3 tablespoons lemon juice and ½ cup water for the orange juice, and 1 teaspoon grated lemon rind for the orange rind.

Sabayon Sauce

6 egg yolks
¾ cup sugar
¾ cup Marsala or sweet sherry
2 tablespoons cherry liqueur
1 cup heavy cream, whipped

Beat the egg yolks and sugar in the top of a double boiler until light in color. Mix in the wine; place over hot water and cook, beating steadily, until mixture is thick. Remove from heat, add the liqueur and beat until mixture is cool. Chill. Fold in the whipped cream just before serving. Serve on cakes or puddings or as directed in recipes.

Makes about 4 cups.

Chocolate Sauce

3 squares (3 ounces) unsweetened chocolate
½ cup water
¼ cup sugar
⅛ teaspoon salt
2 tablespoons butter
1 teaspoon vanilla extract

Cook the chocolate and water over low heat until chocolate is melted, stirring almost constantly. Mix in the sugar and salt until sugar dissolves. Beat in the butter and vanilla. Serve hot or cold with soufflés, cakes or ice cream.

Makes about ¾ cup.

Vanilla Sauce

5 egg yolks
½ cup sugar
2 teaspoons cornstarch
⅛ teaspoon salt
2 cups light cream, scalded
1½ teaspoons vanilla extract

In the top of a double boiler, beat the egg yolks, sugar, cornstarch and salt. Gradually add the hot cream, stirring continuously. Place over hot water and cook, stirring constantly until mixture coats the spoon. Strain and mix in the vanilla. Cool, mixing occasionally. Serve with cake or fruits.

Makes about 2½ cups.

VARIATION

Vanilla Cream Sauce: Fold ½ cup whipped cream into the Vanilla Sauce.

French Sauce

1 cup heavy cream
1 cup sliced strawberries
2 tablespoons cognac
1 cup Vanilla Sauce

Whip the cream. Lightly mash the strawberries with the cognac. Fold the whipped cream and berries into the Vanilla Sauce. Chill. Serve on cakes or ice cream.

Makes about 2½ cups.

Sauce Parisienne

1 cup strawberries
2 tablespoons cognac
1 cup Vanilla Sauce
1 cup heavy cream, whipped

Mash the berries with the cognac. Fold into the Vanilla Sauce with the whipped cream. Serve with fruits, puddings or soufflés.

Makes 3 cups.

Ice Cream Sauce

½ pint vanilla ice cream
1 cup heavy cream, whipped
3 tablespoons cognac, rum or fruit liqueur (optional)

Soften the ice cream slightly, then fold in the cream (and liqueur, if you like). Serve with puddings, soufflés *beignets.*

Makes about 2½ cups.

Berry Sauce

2 cups strawberries or raspberries, fresh or frozen
¼ to ½ cup sugar
1 tablespoon lemon juice
2 teaspoons cornstarch
2 tablespoons cognac

Cook the berries, sugar (½ cup for fresh, ¼ cup for frozen) and lemon juice until soft, about 10 minutes. Force through a sieve. Mix the cornstarch and cognac together until smooth. Add to the hot fruit juice; cook the mixture over low heat, stirring constantly, until it is clear and thickened. Sauce may be served hot or cold. Serve with fruits, soufflés or ice cream.

Makes about 1¼ cups.

Jubilee Sauce

1 No. 2 can pitted black Bing cherries
2 teaspoons cornstarch
¼ cup cognac

Drain the cherries, reserving 1 cup of the juice. Mix the cornstarch and juice together in a saucepan; cook over low heat, stirring constantly until clear and thickened. Add the cherries. Warm the cognac and set it aflame. Add to the sauce. Serve with ice cream or puddings.

Makes about 2 cups.

Foamy Sauce

2 egg yolks
1 cup sifted confectioners' sugar
1 teaspoon vanilla extract
½ cup heavy cream, whipped
2 egg whites, stiffly beaten

Beat the egg yolks until thick, then gradually beat in the confectioners' sugar until light and frothy. Stir in the vanilla. Fold in the whipped cream, then the egg whites. Serve cold with puddings or soufflés.

Makes about 1½ cups.

Caramel Sauce

1 cup water
1 cup sugar
¾ cup heavy cream

Cook the water and sugar together until syrupy and caramel-colored. Remove from heat and place saucepan in cold water to prevent burning. Stir in the cream. Serve hot or cold with puddings or ice cream.

Makes about 1¼ cups.

Apricot Sauce

2 cups apricot jam
1 cup water
2 tablespoons sugar
¼ cup Cointreau or Curaçao

Cook the jam, water and sugar together over low heat 10 minutes, stirring frequently. Force through a sieve. Stir in the liqueur. Serve with fritters, ice cream or fruits.

Makes about 2 cups.

Hard Sauce

¼ pound sweet butter
½ cup sifted confectioners' sugar
2 tablespoons cognac, rum or sweet sherry

Cream the butter, then gradually beat in the sugar until light and fluffy. Add the liqueur ½ teaspoon at a time, beating well. Chill. Serve with puddings.

Makes about 1 cup.

Conversion Chart

for Weights, Measures, and Temperature

WEIGHT EQUIVALENTS

AMERICAN & BRITISH	FRENCH
1 ounce	30 grams
2 ounces	60 grams
8 ounces	240 grams
1 pound	480 grams

LIQUID EQUIVALENTS

AMERICAN		BRITISH		FRENCH
¼ cup	=	2 ounces	=	0.56 deciliters
⅓ cup	=	2½ ounces	=	0.75 deciliters
½ cup	=	4 ounces	=	1.13 deciliters
⅔ cup	=	5 ounces	=	1.5 deciliters
¾ cup	=	6 ounces	=	1.68 deciliters
1 cup	=	8 ounces	=	2.27 deciliters
2 cups	=	16 ounces	=	4.5 deciliters
1 quart	=	32 ounces	=	9 deciliters

OTHER EQUIVALENTS

AMERICAN & BRITISH	FRENCH
1 pinch	1 pincée
1 teaspoon	1 cuillère à café
1 tablespoon	1 cuillère à soupe

TEMPERATURE EQUIVALENTS

AMERICAN (Fahrenheit)	BRITISH (Regular)—Fahrenheit	FRENCH (Centigrade)
225°	# ¾	Doux 107
250°		
275°	# ½	
300°	# 1 (291°)	Moyen 140
325°	# 2 (313°)	
350°	# 3 (336°)	Assez Chaud 177
	# 4 (358°)	
375°	# 5 (379°)	
400°	# 6 (403°)	
425°	# 7 (424°)	Chaud 210
450°	# 8 (446°)	
475°	# 9 (469°)	Très Chaud 246

Index

HB5C